The Clergy Club

John Crothers

The Clergy Club

John Crothers

Adelaide
2018

Cover design by Myf Cadwallader.

ISBN: 978-1-925643-87-9 (paperback)
         978-1-925643-88-6 (hardback)
         978-1-925643-89-3 (epub)
         978-1-925643-90-9 (pdf)

Text Mino Pros Size 10&11.

Published by:

An imprint of the ATF Press Publishing
Group owned by ATF (Australia) Ltd.
PO Box 504
Hindmarsh, SA 5007
ABN 90 116 359 963
www.atfpress.com
Making a lasting impact

Table of Contents

Preface

The Day I Joined the Club

My ordination Mass took place at St Mary's Cathedral on a warm Saturday morning in January 1985. The Cathedral was filled with family, friends and well-wishers, with more than one hundred and fifty priests and bishops concelebrating. It was celebrated with all the pomp and ceremony usually associated with an ordination Mass. I was excited, nervous and overwhelmed, all at the same time, and much of the ceremony passed in a blur. But there was one thing in particular that I do remember well, and that was something that took place during the sign of peace, just before Communion.

At an ordination Mass, the newly ordained priests are involved in a rather extended sign of peace, being greeted by all the priests and bishops who are concelebrating the Mass. It is a very moving experience. I knew many of those priests well. Some were class mates and fellow seminarians. Others were older priests who had supported me along the journey. Some were personal friends with whom I had shared much.

As I moved from one to the other I received many hand-shakes, many awkward hugs, and many expressions of congratulations and support. But it was one greeting in particular that has always stuck in my mind, uttered by a priest with a big, beaming smile who put his hand on my shoulder and said, 'Welcome to the Club'.

Even with everything else that was going on in my head at the time, I remember those words jarring. They were certainly not intended to have any negative overtones. It was a simple expression of welcome and acceptance. But those words have always stuck in my mind, and I remember thinking at the time that whatever model of priesthood I live out in the future, I hope it has nothing to do with a priestly club.

Introduction

Many books and articles have been written about what is often referred to as 'clericalism' in the Catholic Church. It is a subject that is constantly talked about in Church circles, both among the laity and the clergy themselves. But what exactly is 'clericalism'?

The term has various meanings, and many interpretations. In its most general sense, it refers simply to clerical principles and clerical influence. In a more specific sense it refers to clerical power, and the attempts that are made to uphold that power. Another meaning of the word, which is popular today, incorporates a notion of exaggerated self-importance on behalf of the clergy.

One particular description of clericalism, which I feel sums up the phenomenon well, comes from Archbishop Timothy Costelloe, currently archbishop of Perth. In 2008 Archbishop Costelloe gave a talk to the clergy of the Archdiocese of Canberra and Goulburn in which he addressed the topic of clericalism in the Church. In his talk he had this to say. 'Let me say at once that in my own mind "clericalism" has little or nothing to do with what priests wear or what they ask people to call them. It has to do with an attitude of superiority or aloofness which conveys the impression that priests are better than others, holier than others, somehow or other removed from others, precisely because priests deal with things of God, sacred things, as opposed to the laity, who deal with worldly or secular things. And from this attitude flows the expectation that priests should be treated with special deference, with a special privilege, with a level of respect that others don't really deserve.'[1]

---

1. Bishop Timothy Costelloe SDB, 'Applying a Pauline Theology of Priesthood', *The Priest* (the Journal of the Australian Confraternity of Catholic Clergy), 24/11 (May 2009): 9.

This is the type of clericalism I am referring to in this book, although I use another phrase to describe the phenomenon. I call it the 'the clergy club mentality'. In the following pages I will attempt to define exactly what this mentality is, to find out where it comes from, to see how it expresses itself, and, of course, to see how it can be transformed into something more positive and uplifting for the Church.

About the Author

You cannot write a book, any book, from a totally objective perspective. Who we are, how we act, what we think, are all influenced by everything around us, and by all the varied experiences we have. The people in our lives, our upbringing, the things that happen to us, our successes, and our failures, all leave their mark, and all have an effect on how we see life, how we see God, and how we see each other.

It is for this reason that I begin this book with a few words about myself. My views on Church and priesthood have not come out of a vacuum. I am a product of my era, my family, my friends, my life experiences, my Church experiences, my priesthood experiences, and everything else that has impacted on my life over the past sixty-seven years.

I was born in Sydney in 1951 and for the first fifteen years of my life our family home was at Ashfield. I was blessed with a wonderful, loving family and a very happy childhood. We were a traditional Catholic family of the 1950s and 60s. The parish was the centre of our faith life, and also the focal point for our social life. We went to Mass every Sunday and attended most of the other parish activities, from benediction to parish picnics. The majority of Catholic families in the area knew each other through the Church, and all my friends were Catholic.

At home, we regularly said the rosary in the evenings, and we often had discussions about religion around the dinner table. My father was a traditional conservative Catholic of his era. Whatever the pope said had to be right. On the other hand, the children in the family were growing up in the era of the Beatles and Vatican II. Needless to say, there was little agreement between Dad and us kids on what the Church should, or should not, be doing. I did not realise it then, but those dinner table discussions were an expression of two very different models of Church, the pre-Vatican Council model and the post-Vatican Council model, two perspectives which still today challenge each other, and provide a healthy tension within the broader Church community.

My school years were unremarkable. I attended the parish primary school from kindergarten to year 6 and then the local Catholic high school from year 7 to year 12. Academically I never stood out, but I always managed to get through the exams. During my high school years I was probably more interested in music, sport, and getting to know the girls at the high school next door, than I was in study. I had always loved music, and in my teenage years I started playing in rock bands like so many teenagers of my era, all hoping to become superstars. I still remember the first time I played on stage. It was at a school dance in the parish hall, and it was packed with young people from around the area. Singing and playing guitar in the band was about the coolest thing you could do at the time.

After completing year 12, I went to the University of New South Wales to do a Bachelor of Arts and a Diploma in Education, with the intention of becoming a schoolteacher. With one semester of my University course to go I decided to live on campus, to cut back on travel time. I found some accommodation at Warrane College, a residential college run by the Catholic institution known as *Opus Dei*.

My time at Warrane was a very rewarding experience for me. There was a chapel in the college and I used to spend regular quiet time there. It was the first time, certainly in many years, that I had ever stopped and really prayed. I had always gone to Sunday Mass but until that time I had never really personalised my faith. I also had a number of chats with one of the priests at the college who helped me significantly in thinking about where my life was heading.

That experience at Warrane College certainly had an influence on my decision to go to the seminary the following year, and begin my training for the priesthood at St Columba's College Seminary at Springwood. There were thirty-four of us who started together in February 1974. We were from all different parts of NSW, and we were all young. In fact, at twenty-two years of age, I was the second oldest in the group.

Seminary life is challenging, but also very rewarding. I studied hard, prayed hard, made life-time friends, and grew enormously as a person. In 1978, however, half way through my fifth year in the seminary, I started to question whether I should continue. It was not that

I had lost my desire to be a priest, but rather, I was trying to decide whether I may be more suited to marriage and family life. And so, I made the decision to leave the seminary, although I always knew that as long as I kept an open mind to the future, eventually things would make themselves clear. And they did. Four and a half years later, in February 1983, I returned to the seminary to complete my studies, and was ordained to the priesthood in January 1985.

These past thirty-three years as a priest have been truly wonderful years. I have lived and worked in numerous parishes in Sydney, met many wonderful people, experienced many grace-filled moments, and been challenged and affirmed, loved and supported. I was also given the opportunity to study in Rome for two years, when I was in my early forties. It was a truly enriching experience and another factor, among many, that has influenced the way I see the world, the Church, and the priesthood.

Finally, I believe that the experience of priesthood has made me a better person. By that, I am not saying that ordination has made me a better person, but rather, through the experiences I have had in priestly ministry, and particularly through the many generous and faith-filled people who have touched my life, I have been challenged to be the best person I can be, even if I don't always measure up to that challenge.

Clergy Culture

One of the things that has always troubled me, since the day I was ordained, is why the clergy do not get on better with the laity. I guess I just always expected that priests working in parishes would have a very close relationship with their parishioners, particularly with those who are more actively involved in the life of the parish. I just assumed that they would be happy to support them in their ministry, treat them as fellow workers, advocate for them where necessary, and generally have a pleasant, friendly relationship with them.

I soon found out that in many cases this is far from reality. In fact, quite often the opposite is the case. Underlying tensions between priests and parishioners are frequently evident. Sometimes the clergy feel threatened by the laity, especially by those who are more actively involved in the parish, or working in parish ministries. They can find it difficult to see the laity as fellow workers or to advocate on their behalf.

An 'us and them' mentality can develop. The attitude of the clergy towards the laity can even come across as condescending or rude.

I know some will say that I am exaggerating, or even proposing a concept that doesn't exist. Obviously, the clergy will be defensive. No one likes to be criticised, especially those in leadership positions. Some of the laity, too, will argue against a clergy club mentality. Many Catholics do not like the Church being held to account or being criticised in any way, particularly by one of its own. But many others, including some members of the clergy, say that the topic needs to be addressed.

There are no names mentioned in this book. There is no attempt in any way to criticise any member of the clergy, or even the clergy generally. As a member of the clergy myself I am part of the problem. I have acted and spoken in ways that have been far from inclusive and welcoming. We all have.

But the real reason that there are no names mentioned in this book is that the problem is fundamentally an institutional problem, a structural problem. Priests come and go. Bishops come and go. But the clergy club mentality will remain until it is addressed, and steps are taken to eradicate it.

I am sure some people, particularly among the clergy, will see this book as a criticism of the priesthood, or of priests themselves. That is certainly not my intention. Yes, I cite many examples of situations where priests and bishops could have acted with a greater sense of humility and service, but the criticism is fundamentally a criticism of a system that excuses, and indeed reinforces, this type of behaviour.

One could genuinely ask, 'But what about all the good things that priests do, and all the wonderful priests who have done so much for so many people?' I totally agree. Every group has its bad apples, but in my opinion the vast majority of priests are hard-working, good-hearted people, who have gone into the priesthood with the best of motives, and have done an enormous amount of good for the Catholic community, and beyond. But even so, the clergy club mentality is still a reality, and clericalism has to be addressed.

I must say also, that I write as a diocesan priest who, apart from a couple of years in Rome, has worked only in the Sydney Archdiocese. That is my experience of priesthood, but I would be surprised if much of what is said in the book does not resonate with Catholic clergy in other dioceses, and indeed in other countries, as well as with priests in religious orders and religious communities.

Content of the Book

I admit the title of this book is somewhat provocative. It does con-
jure up images of separation and exclusiveness on the part of the
clergy. But this is exactly my thesis, that the ordained ministers of
the Church have in fact become separate and exclusive, disconnected
from the laity, in a way that is preventing both the laity, and the clergy
themselves, from flourishing as they should.

The book covers a lot of topics, from celibacy to contraception,
from liturgical language to gluten-free altar breads, and many other
topics in between. The reason the content of the book is so broad is
that the clergy club mentality itself is so far-reaching. Because bishops
and priests have such a prominent and influential role in the Church,
the way they think affects just about every aspect of the Church's life.

There are five parts to the book. Part 1 looks at what exactly the
clergy club is. Is there really a disconnect between clergy and laity? In
what way do priests and bishops think differently to the laity? How do
their priorities differ? How do their interpretations of the Scriptures
differ? How do the day to day experiences of the clergy differ from
those of the people in the pews? And how do these differences help to
bring about a particular mentality?

Part 2 asks the question 'Where does the clergy club mentality
come from?' How does seminary training contribute to the club
mentality? How does traditional Catholic theology of priesthood
influence the way the clergy see themselves? How does the fact that
Catholic priests and bishops are almost exclusively male and celibate,
at least in the Latin rite, influence the way they see the world?

Part 3 then looks at the way the clergy club mentality expresses
itself in the Church, and beyond. Is it true that priests tend to speak
and act in a way that supports and reinforces the institutional Church?
Is there pressure on the clergy to conform, to agree with the views
of the incumbent bishop, and to fit in with his particular model of
Church? Is there resistance to change within the clergy? Is there a
tendency towards legalism? Is it true that the clergy tend to be very
forgiving of their own colleagues, but take a harder stance against
those not in the club?

Part 4 focusses on the Gospels, and in particular, on the way that
Jesus exercised his own ministry, how he related to those around him,
how he connected with both the clergy and the laity of his day. Jesus
is the model for all Christians, in all things. His ministry is the model

for all Christian vocations, including priesthood. It is important, therefore, that the clergy view their own ministry through the prism of Jesus' ministry, and see how closely the two fit together.

The final part of the book, Part 5, is titled 'A Way Forward'. Here I look at ways that priests and laity together, can find a greater sense of connectedness and solidarity. In particular, I look at ways that clergy can develop a more inclusive and welcoming approach to the laity, as well as becoming more open to notions of accountability and change. I also propose eight practical changes that I believe would help to break down the clergy club mentality. None of these changes is incompatible with Church doctrine or any of the principles of our faith. They are all very doable, and if they could be implemented, they would go a long way towards showing that the hierarchy is serious about eradicating from the Church, what Pope Francis calls, 'one of the worst evils'.[2]

Why I Have Written this Book

The idea of writing this book has been on my mind for many years. In fact, ever since I was ordained I have been reflecting on the relationship between the laity and the clergy. I have often been saddened, sometimes shocked, by the way members of the clergy have treated the laity. I have sat with people in tears who have had shattering experiences with priests. I have tried to keep a balanced approach to these situations. I know there are two sides to every story, and I have tried to be careful not to be judgemental or rush to hasty conclusions. But the number of times these situations have occurred have been far too numerous to ignore. Coupled with my own experience of stories told by fellow clergy, I am now totally convinced that priests and bishops treat the laity in a very different manner to the way they treat their own colleagues. This is at the heart of what I call the 'clergy club mentality'.

And so, I need to say something about this blight on the priesthood. As a priest myself, I feel I am able to say it, because I too am caught up in the whole clergy club culture. I speak as one who belongs

---

2. From a question and answer session during a meeting between Pope Francis and 120 superiors of religious orders held on 29 November 2013, published in *La Civilta Cattolica* on 27 December 2013.

to a very elite clerical group. I speak as one who, for decades, has been placed on a pedestal. I speak as one who has been constantly told how important he is. I speak as one who is part of the club.

It is not easy for me to write a book that is clearly critical of the institutional Church, and in particular, critical of the priesthood that I belong to. The Church has been a part of my life since I was baptised, at the very tender age of two weeks. It has been a constant source of inspiration and challenge throughout those years. I owe a great debt of gratitude to the vocation of priesthood that has brought me so much fulfilment, joy and satisfaction in life. But sometimes things need to be said, whether it's about the priesthood, the Church, or society in general. In particular, I write this book for the many members of the Catholic community who have become disappointed, disillusioned, or angry with the Church, because of what they see as elitism, or arrogance, on the part of the clergy.

I also write this book in order to present a picture of what I believe the priesthood could be, with all its great potential to be a life giving, and love giving force in the world, a potential that I feel is not being fully realised at the present time. There is so much goodwill among the laity. Indeed, the love, support and care that parishioners show towards their priests is quite extraordinary. But a club mentality on the part of the clergy can, over time, seriously damage that relationship. And sadly, that is exactly what is happening at the moment.

If this book can get one priest or bishop thinking about his relationship with the laity in a more positive and open way, then I will feel that my efforts have been worthwhile.

Two Practical Issues

Before moving on, I need to mention two practical issues that have presented somewhat of a dilemma in terms of how I write this book. First, as a priest myself, I should be using words such as 'we' and 'us' when referring to the clergy. I am part of the clergy, and indeed I share in the clergy club mentality. But it becomes very difficult in terms of literary style, to be constantly writing in the first person, and having to qualify every reference to the clergy with some form of 'me included'. So, I have decided that most of the time I will refer to the clergy in the third person, to make the style more agreeable, but

I stress that I am in no way disassociating myself from the clergy, or from the clerical mentality and culture that I am challenging.

The second issue relates to the nature and role of deacons, and it is a somewhat more complicated matter.

When we think of ordination in the Catholic Church we tend to think only of ordination to the priesthood. But the deacon is also ordained, as is the bishop. The three ordinations together constitute what is traditionally called 'Holy Orders'. The deacon receives the first of the orders when he is ordained to the diaconate, and it is through this ordination that he formally becomes a member of the Catholic clergy, and so, technically, a member of 'the club'.

Unlike priests and bishops, however, deacons can exercise their ministry either on a temporary basis, or on a permanent basis. A student for the priesthood becomes a temporary deacon when, usually about twelve months or so out from his priestly ordination, he is invited to be ordained to the diaconate. He will then exercise this ministry for a short period of time until his ordination to the priesthood. This practice is based on the principle that one has to be a deacon before becoming a priest, just as one has to be a priest before becoming a bishop.

But there are also those who are ordained to the diaconate, not as a step towards priesthood, but rather to exercise their ministry as deacons for the rest of their lives. While, like priests and bishops, the deacon is part of the clergy, there are some fundamental differences between the role of the permanent deacon on the one hand, and the role of priests and bishops on the other. For instance, the permanent deacon does not take a vow of celibacy, and consequently many of them are married with families. Also, they often exercise their ministry on a part-time basis while pursuing another career. As well, deacons are not remunerated by the Church in the same way that priests and bishops are.

Because of these differences, and especially the fact that permanent deacons do not take a vow of celibacy, I would argue that they do not share the clergy club mentality in the same way that other members of the clergy do, since their life styles are so different. Indeed, I would suggest that the life style of the married deacon is more akin to that of the laity than it is to the life style of the priest or bishop. In any case, I have found that much of what I have to say about the clergy club mentality does not apply to permanent deacons, at least in the same way that it applies to the rest of the clergy, and for this reason I have decided to focus only on those members of the clergy who are priests and bishops. So, when I refer to 'the clergy', it is only bishops and priests that I am referring to. I know this is not a perfect solution by any means, but it is the only practical way that I feel I can deal with the issue. I do hope the permanent deacons understand my dilemma.

Part 1
What is the Clergy Club?

The term 'club' has many meanings. There are formal clubs such as an RSL club or a golf club where membership is clearly defined, with club members paying an annual fee and given a membership number, and expected to follow the rules of the club. There are certain privileges given to club members but there are also sanctions for those who do not keep up the standards.

Then there are less formal clubs such as a book club or a social club, where membership is more fluid and the rules more relaxed. But even in these looser associations there are certain expectations on members to support the common values of the group and to not cause disunity among the members.

Then there are associations where the term club is used in a more metaphorical sense. The term 'boys' club' is a typical example. It does refer to a particular group of people, perhaps a group of work colleagues or a faction in a political party, but the real emphasis is on the attitude of the members. The 'club' notion represents more a mentality rather than the specific individuals in the group.

This is the way I use the term in reference to the clergy club. It refers to an attitude or a mentality rather than to the actual people who make up the clergy. Priests and bishops come and go, but the mentality remains, because it is supported by the structures and the institution itself.

I was once talking to a priest who for some years had been on the staff of one of the seminaries in Australia. He was telling me that he and other members of the staff were constantly amazed by how quickly the new seminarians became institutionalised and clericalised. He said it took only a few weeks for a new seminarian to take on the attitudes and values of the group.

So, what exactly is the clergy club mentality?

Put in its simplest form, the clergy club mentality is an attitude of exaggerated self-importance and exclusiveness on the part of bishops and priests.

It sounds a bit harsh, but in reality it is so easy for this to happen. Perhaps one has to actually be a member of the clergy to understand how subtle and how seductive is the temptation for a priest to see himself as more important than members of the laity. From the moment you are ordained everyone treats you differently. You are put on a pedestal and told how wonderful you are. Even other priests and bishops treat you differently. You have instant status, authority and power, and an enormous amount of influence over people's lives. You don't earn it, you are just given it, by virtue of the fact that you have been ordained to the priesthood.

I remember at the conclusion of my ordination Mass, after we had processed back into the cathedral sacristy, the archbishop came over to me, knelt down on one knee in front of me, and asked for my blessing. Clearly something had changed quite dramatically from the time we entered the cathedral.

The Image of the Priest

One thing that has been said to me many times over the years is the statement 'You don't look like a priest'. I am certainly not the only priest who has had this said to him, but it does raise the question, 'What does a priest "look like?"'

The image that people have of the priest obviously varies enormously. One day after Mass a woman suggested to me that I should be wearing a clerical collar. 'You don't look like a priest', she said, 'you look like an ordinary man'. Obviously, her image of the priest was of someone quite different and removed from 'ordinary' people. This attitude is not uncommon, particularly among more traditional Catholics.

On the other hand, many people today do want their priest to 'look like an ordinary man'. They certainly want him to be a good leader, and teacher, to be imbued with the person of Jesus and the values of the Gospel, but they also want to feel relaxed with him, and to know that he is relaxed with them, and understands where they are coming from.

Much of this of course, is cultural. Many Catholics born overseas have grown up in a country where the priest has a privileged position in society. It is only natural that this would continue to influence their image of the priest. In the same way those who have grown up in an egalitarian society such as Australia, would feel much more at ease with priests and bishops who are more down to earth. But I can't help feeling that no matter what one's cultural background may be, or indeed, what one's image of the priest may be, in the vast majority of cases the laity want a priest who is not distant, but is someone they can relate to. And it is not easy relating to a priest with a club mentality.

Clergy/Lay Disconnect

The fundamental thesis of this book is that there is a disconnection between clergy and laity in the Church, that this disconnection is a direct result of the clergy club mentality, and it needs to be urgently addressed and resolved.

I admit that there would be some among the laity who would not have experienced this disconnection. It is not something that would be always obvious to the outside observer, and especially to those who have had no personal dealings with priests and bishops. Moreover, in most cases the laity do not protest about the difficulties they might be enduring with their pastors. Perhaps, too, a remoteness on the part of the clergy has been so much part of the culture of the Church that for many people it is just a given. Also, there is so much good will on the part of the laity towards their priests that mostly they just grin and bear it.

I am sure, too, there are some people who would say 'Yes, the disconnection between the clergy and the laity does exist, but it should exist'. They would see priests and bishops as very different from the laity, and would argue that this difference, this separation, should be respected and maintained. Indeed, there are some who believe that one of the problems with the Church today is that many priests want to 'bring themselves down' to the level of the laity.

But there are other members of the laity, and particularly those who are more actively involved in the life of the Church, who are becoming more and more frustrated by a clerical culture that they see as exclusive, rigid, and not supportive of the role of the laity in the Church.

It is also true that many members of the clergy feel somewhat threatened by the laity and their role in the Church. For sixteen years I was parish priest of a parish that had been set up in the 1980s as the first parish in Sydney to have a non-resident parish priest. It was, and is, a wonderful parish where the parishioners are very involved in all areas of parish life and have a great sense of ownership of their ministries. Yet there was a feeling among many priests that they did not want to work in the parish, because the parishioners were 'running the parish', as they put it. Of course, this was not true. The leadership and sacramental roles of the priest were the same as in any parish, but I could never understand why so many of the clergy could not celebrate the active participation of the parish community. There was certainly nothing to be afraid of, and much to celebrate and enjoy.

Religious Culture

Culture, in general, is such an extraordinary thing. It plays a huge part in how we think, how we act and what our priorities are in life. Religious culture, too, has an enormous influence on how we see the world. I am writing a book about the Catholic priesthood because I was born in a Christian country, and in a Catholic family. But if I had been born in Israel or Iran, for instance, I may well be still writing a book about religious leadership, but it probably would not have anything to do with the Catholic priesthood.

Those of us who are members of the Church, particularly if we were born into it, have a view of the world that is profoundly affected by the values and the principles of the Church. We grew up with the stories of our faith, stories about Jesus, stories about Adam and Eve, stories about miracles and angels, plagues and floods. We have seen popes and cardinals come and go, each with his own particular slant on the Catholic faith. Those of us who are old enough to remember, have seen both a pre-Vatican II Church, and a post-Vatican II Church, with their various similarities and differences. These elements, and more, make up the myriad of factors that comprise our broad religious culture. Priests and bishops share this culture like everyone else, but they also experience another religious sub-culture which is perhaps even more influential—the clergy culture.

Clerical Solidarity

The clergy culture has many features, one of which is a very strong bond that exists between members of the clergy. Priests and bishops comprise a very small percentage of the population, and that in itself probably brings its own sense of solidarity. In addition, the clergy share a lot in common, in terms of ministry and everyday experiences. They do things that only priests and bishops do, like celebrating Mass and hearing confessions. They listen to people sharing their innermost secrets, and are invited into the privacy of their lives. It is something that very few people experience.

The vow of celibacy is another thing that priests have in common. Making a life-time promise not to marry is a rather unusual thing to do, to say the least, particularly in this modern day and age. It puzzles many people. Some see it as a positive commitment, while others see it as quite unnatural, and odd, or even selfish. But whatever the views about celibacy, those who have made the decision to take it on, certainly share a common experience, an experience that is intrinsic to the way they live their lives.

There is another thing that priests share together, and that is an expectation placed on them that their religious views will be in lock-step with the views of the Church hierarchy. While pressure to be orthodox is not something unique to the clergy, it is certainly true that for many priests, and also for some bishops, there is a constant tension between, on the one hand, being honest to their own views and perspectives on faith and life, while on the other hand, not wishing to upset the Church authorities, either locally or in Rome. It is a tension that many of the clergy live with for years, some for the whole of their lives. It is relevant to the notion of clerical solidarity because many priests feel they can only speak openly when they are 'among friends'.

The bonding that priests and bishops share together is a very admirable trait, and for many of the clergy it provides a great source of support and comfort. But it can be a short step from a sense of solidarity with the group, to a mentality that is inward-looking and exclusive. This is the constant danger facing all members of the clergy, from the day they are ordained.

Clubs Everywhere

A club mentality is certainly not unique to the priesthood. Every profession, every occupation, has its 'clergy' and 'laity', and potentially a disconnection between the two. I have heard comments, for example, from nurses working in hospitals that the doctors can be quite dismissive of their suggestions regarding a patient's care. Given that the nurse has been looking after the patient on a daily basis, the doctor's attitude is probably more indicative of a 'doctors' club' mentality, than it is of the quality of the nurse's advice.

Not long ago I was talking to a man who was a minister in a Protestant denomination. I mentioned that I was writing a book on clericalism, and he wanted to know more. After we had been chatting for a while he said to me, 'Don't worry, there's clericalism in our denomination too'.

I am sure, if the truth be known, there is a club mentality in most, if not all occupations and professions, where those in leadership positions have an exaggerated sense of their own importance, and tend to be distant and exclusive in their attitude to others.

Leadership in the Church

While I am arguing for less emphasis on the distinction between clergy and laity, I am certainly not suggesting that there are no differences between the two groups. Each has its own specific character, and its own distinctive role. In particular, the clergy are entrusted with a leadership role in the Church which they exercise in a unique way. Indeed, I believe it is the very notion of leadership that defines priesthood at its most fundamental level. As someone who has exercised that leadership role at the parish level over many years I can say that it is a most fulfilling, rewarding, and enjoyable ministry, and one that can only be described as an absolute privilege to exercise.

Traditionally, clerical leadership in the Church has been defined under the headings of 'Teacher, Priest and Shepherd'. As teacher, the priest or bishop informs, instructs and inspires the community, reinforcing the message of Jesus' own teaching, and expressing it in terms of Catholic faith. In practice, he does this through his homilies at Mass and other liturgies, through formal talks and instructions, and through the many informal ways that the priest teaches the Gospel message.

As priest, he offers the Eucharistic sacrifice of the Mass on behalf of the whole community. The Mass is the high point of Catholic worship, and the priest's role in leading that worship is central to his ministry. As an extension of that priestly role he leads the prayer in the various other liturgical celebrations.

As shepherd, he exercises the pastoral dimension of leadership, showing care and compassion for the community, and a listening ear to those in need. In practice, he does this by celebrating the healing sacraments of Reconciliation and Anointing of the Sick, comforting the elderly, supporting those burdened with problems and challenges, and through any other way he can expresses the love and compassion of Jesus.

Leadership from Within

The Teacher-Priest-Shepherd model of Church leadership is indeed a beautiful, challenging and multi-dimensional expression of the leadership of Jesus, as exercised by the bishops and priests in the Church. But it is only effective when it is internalised in the leader himself, when it becomes a leadership of the heart, and not just a leadership of the head.

Some time ago a bishop had been celebrating Mass in a parish where I had once been appointed, and his theme for the homily was humility. Over the following weeks I had occasion to meet a number of parishioners who had attended the Mass, and I was struck by one particular comment they consistently made. They could not reconcile the fact that the bishop wore a mitre while he was preaching on humility. I am sure the bishop would have given a good theological reason why it was appropriate for him to wear a mitre while preaching, but the fact remains that his message was lost, and his teaching role diminished, due to a perceived inconsistency between his words and actions.

In a similar way, the sacrificial, priestly dimension of leadership is also dependent on how it is embodied in the person of the leader. A parishioner who attended a Mass where the priest took an excessive amount of time to purify the chalice and ciborium after Communion, made the comment that 'it was all about him'. Once again, I am sure the priest concerned would argue that it was totally appropriate to spend a lot of time purifying the sacred vessels, but surely if a priest

Disconnection from the Real World

Most priests live in a bubble, a clerical bubble. They do not experience a lot of things that the laity do, even with regard to the day-to-day chores of life. In many cases, if not the majority of cases, someone cooks for them, cleans for them, and even washes their clothes. I have always found it incongruous that people who claim to be called to a life of service can accept such a situation, and even expect it.

Of course, it could be argued that the priest's life is a very busy one, and they simply don't have time for such mundane tasks. I would argue instead, however, that having someone wait on you in this way, particularly for a young priest who comes to his first parish, can only sow the seeds of elitism, and lay the groundwork for the clergy club mentality.

This disconnection from the real world can also be seen in a clerical attitude that judges the laity much more harshly than it judges the clergy. Some years ago, a bishop suggested publicly that people who divorce should pay a divorce tax, to compensate for the harm done to society when families separate.[5] Of course, no one wants to see divorce on the increase, but to me the bishop's statement suggests that he has little appreciation of the challenges and complexities of married life, or family relationships. I am sure that if the suggestion were made that the Church should pay a special tax for the damage done to society by the crimes of priests, it would not go down well with the hierarchy.

Once again, I stress that I say this not to be critical, but to show how easily the clergy can say things that seem completely out of touch with the real world. This is brought about by their disconnection from the laity, and from many of the normal experiences of life, a disconnection that sees them looking at the world from a very limited, and 'churchy' perspective.

This disconnection can also be seen at the liturgical level. In January 2007 guidelines were issued to the priests of the Sydney Archdiocese, informing the clergy that eulogies at funeral Masses were forbidden, in accordance with the new Order of Christian Funerals.[6] The argument is that 'the Funeral Mass is an act of worship and

---

5. 'Pell Speaks out on Divorce Laws', *The Catholic Weekly*, 60/4078 (2 September 2001): 1.
6. 'Guidelines For Speaking in Remembrance of the Dead', Archdiocese of Sydney, 13 January 2007.

prayer that should not admit elements foreign to its intrinsic nature'. But to me, the idea that the story of a deceased person's life cannot be intertwined with the story of Jesus' life, or worse, that the story of a person's life is 'foreign' to the intrinsic nature of Christian worship and prayer, goes against the whole notion of the Incarnation, which expresses and celebrates the coming together of the human and the divine.

Club Loyalty

Loyalty is a wonderful virtue. When someone is prepared to show constant and steadfast allegiance to another person, or even to a particular cause, it is something very admirable. Priests and bishops show great loyalty to each other, and this is to be admired and supported. But the dynamics of the institution are strong, and care must be taken that the genuine loyalty experienced between priests and bishops does not develop into what could be termed a misguided loyalty.

When the word 'loyalty' is used in reference to the Church it is usually used in a one-directional sense. The laity are loyal to their priests, the priests are loyal to the bishop, and the bishops are loyal to the pope. Rarely do we hear the pope expressing loyalty to the clergy, or the bishops expressing loyalty to the priests, and almost never do we hear the priests expressing loyalty to the laity. And yet in any community, particularly one professing Gospel values, loyalty must be reciprocal. The loyalty of the priest to a parishioner is no less important than the loyalty of a parishioner to the priest.

It is true that in the ordination ceremony the deacon, who is to be ordained to the priesthood, promises loyalty to the bishop, and his successors. This promise must be treated with great seriousness, but it is not absolute. Any promise of loyalty to a person must be made in the context of other, competing loyalties. A promise of loyalty to a bishop, for example, must be made in the context of loyalty to the whole Church, loyalty to Gospel values, loyalty to one's family and friends, loyalty to one's parishioners. Sadly, we see all too often what can happen when loyalty to a superior overrides justice and compassion.

I was once involved with a petition about the Third Rite of Reconciliation. A group of parishioners, one evening at a meeting, asked if there was anything they could do to get the bishops to take another look at the Third Rite, and maybe find a way to reintroduce it into the parishes. Out of the discussion came a decision to make a petition available to the parishes in the Sydney Archdiocese, with a view to sending the signatures to the Vatican, with an accompanying letter. We started off in our own two parishes, and had over 900 signatures, before we sent it on to other parishes. Unfortunately, we struggled to get many more signatures, as the priests in the other parishes were unwilling to encourage the petition, even though most of them were in support of the Third Rite of Reconciliation. To me it was an example of how the notion of loyalty is seen in a very one-dimensional way by many of the clergy—loyalty to the hierarchy, but not necessarily to the laity.

As a final comment on this topic it should be noted that within the clergy, loyalty can be used, both as a 'carrot', and as a 'stick', to get people to do things they might not otherwise do. As an incentive, loyalty is sometimes used to reward those who follow the party line. For example, a priest who will always do what is asked of him, without questioning, will often be promoted to higher positions. He is seen as 'safe'. On the other hand, a priest who openly questions decisions, or challenges his superiors, is not appointed to positions of responsibility or influence. He is seen as 'unsafe', someone who could not be relied on to toe the party line.

Bishops, too, are subject to this type of treatment. Over the past thirty years we have had some outstanding auxiliary bishops in the Sydney Archdiocese. A number of those bishops, however, while extremely competent and held in high esteem by all, were never entrusted with their own diocese. I can't help feeling that they would have been viewed as 'unsafe' by the authorities in Rome, each having a model of priesthood that was people-orientated, rather than institutional and clerical.

Club Secrecy

One of the criticisms that is often levelled at the Church hierarchy is that they display a lack of transparency, or, as some may describe it, a code of secrecy. There is a sense that bishops feel no responsibility to share information with other members of the Church, even in such areas as administration and finance.

Once, at a clergy meeting, when the topic of the archdiocesan finances came up, I asked the archbishop if he could tell us how much money the archdiocese had in liquid assets, to the nearest ten million dollars. It came as no surprise that the answer was no.

I am sure the archbishop could put forward reasons why he would not want the financial position of the archdiocese made public, but the fact remains that it is something that many organisations are required to do, on the basis that those who are part of the organisation, or who have a vested interest in the organisation, should not be kept in the dark. It also conveys a very positive statement about openness and transparency.

It is rather ironic that at the parish level, the finances have to be made available to all parishioners, and rightly so. It would not be a good look if the parish priest refused to disclose the financial situation of the parish, and it is not a good look when bishops do exactly the same thing at the diocesan level. It simply reinforces the view held by many, that the Church hierarchy act as a law unto themselves, accountable to nobody.

In other areas of the Church's life this code of secrecy is even more worrying. Let's take the example of the way bishops are chosen and appointed. Confidential letters are sent out to certain priests, who are then asked to assess the suitability of a particular candidate. I do not know what weight the priests' assessments are given, or who else is consulted, but it is clear that the whole process takes place behind closed doors. It also ensures that input into the decision is restricted to a few select members of the clergy. The consultation process should be much broader than this, as the appointment of bishops is one of the Church's most important duties.

It is easy to see how this 'in house' way of appointing leaders reinforces the clergy club mentality. Bishops appoint other bishops. The pope appoints the cardinals. The cardinals elect the pope. It's a closed system, a structure that keeps reinforcing itself in such a way that it becomes almost impossible to find a circuit breaker, and so the clerical mentality continues.

Pressure to Conform

In my early years as a priest I was nominated as the representative of the 'young priests group', on a committee that discussed and recommended the appointment of priests to particular parishes. There were five priests in all, who represented the various age groups, and we met about five times a year, together with the archdiocesan bishops, as well as two priests who had a more permanent appointment on the committee.

The first meeting I attended has always remained firmly entrenched in my memory. As we sat around the boardroom table at the cathedral house, I sensed a feeling of anxiety and nervousness among all of us. I do not think any of us felt free to say exactly what we thought. Sometimes the discussions would move beyond issues of particular priests to broader questions about priesthood and Church, but there was constant pressure not to say anything that was controversial. Everyone was expected to toe the party line. The pressure was unspoken, but very real. When someone did speak up, which happened occasionally, you could see that it took an enormous amount of effort and courage to do so.

The reason that this meeting has stayed so clear in my memory is that it was so different to what I was expecting. We were a group of priests and bishops. Surely, we would go to great pains to put each other at ease, to listen to each other's views, and to relate together in a relaxed and friendly way. It did not happen, not because of any wilful intention on the part of the clergy present, but because the institutional structures did not let it happen. It had always been like that, and it was not going to change.

Another example of the pressure on priests to conform can be seen in the introduction of the new translation of the Mass in 2011. A year earlier, in July 2010, I attended the Parramatta Conference of the National Council of Priests. It was a wonderful gathering of priests. One of the topics of discussion was, of course, the new translation, which was soon to be introduced, and which was extremely unpopular among the priests at the conference. Many spoke passionately about the shortcomings of the translation, and what a retrograde step it was to use it in the Mass. In fact, I can honestly say that I have never seen priests as angry about anything as they were about the new translation. Some months later, however, when the time came for it to be introduced into the Mass, it happened with barely a whimper.

There are numerous reasons why priests feel a need to conform. As I mentioned earlier there is a strong sense of loyalty to the bishop. I think there is also a desire to please the bishop, and have him think well of you. There is nothing unusual in that. It is a very natural thing to want to please the boss.

In addition, I believe there is a feeling among many priests that they don't want to 'get into trouble'. I hear it expressed often in general conversation with fellow priests. They use expressions like 'I keep my head down', or 'I make myself a small target'. It is not a sign of a mature relationship between priest and bishop, but it's real for many priests, and one more characteristic of the clergy club mentality.

Diocesan Spirituality

One could not write a book on clericalism, without saying something about the spirituality of the diocesan priest. It is a topic that many diocesan priests have grappled with, as I have, but one that is fundamental to understanding who we are as diocesan priests, and how we relate to the broader Church.

Unlike the spirituality of religious orders, the diocesan spirituality is not easy to describe. There is nothing obvious that defines the diocesan charism. In contrast, if I am a Franciscan priest and someone asks me 'What is Franciscan spirituality about?' I can respond by talking about solidarity with the poor, detachment from material things, emphasis on the goodness and beauty of creation, and so on. In the same way, if I am a Benedictine priest and am asked the same question, I can talk about the contemplative life, listening to the Word of God in the Scriptures, obedience, humility, and so on. They are the things that define what is special about the Franciscan and Benedictine spiritualities, and help to determine the identity of those who belong to the Franciscan and Benedictine communities.

For diocesan priests, however, it is not so easy to articulate. What is it exactly that defines the spirituality of priests who do not belong to a religious order or community?

Often the answers I hear to this question are a bit like 'motherhood' statements. You cannot say they are wrong, but they do not really tell you anything specific about diocesan spirituality. They list such things as fulfilling the role of teacher, priest and shepherd, modelling oneself on the leadership of Christ, being a person of love and service. But these are the qualities of all priests, religious or diocesan.

Sometimes the answer is given as 'Well, the religious order guys are like the specialists, and we diocesan priests are like the general practitioners. We do everything, baptisms, funerals, weddings, sick calls, whatever needs to be done in the local community'. There is certainly truth in that statement, but a spirituality can't be about just what we do. It is about who we are.

I have thought about this issue a lot, and I have come to the conclusion that the thing that defines diocesan spirituality, the thing that makes it unique and special, is our relationship with our parishioners, the people with whom we minister. They are our community. They are the people with whom we live, with whom we learn, with whom we grow.

I hear already the religious order priests saying, 'But our relationship with the people is just as important to us'. No one is denying the importance of the relationship that religious order priests have with their people, or the wonderful work they do in so many different areas, work that I could never do. It is just that we diocesan priests are bonded to our people, by definition. They are our community. We do not have any other.

Sometimes when people ask me where I have worked as a priest, and I tell them, 'Only in Sydney, because that is my diocese', they often seem surprised, expecting that I have worked in other countries, or at least in other parts of Australia. Clearly, they are not aware of the close connection the diocesan priest has with his diocese, and with the people who constitute his diocesan family.

Just recently, after celebrating a Sunday Mass, a woman came up to me and asked, 'Are you a secular priest?' I said 'Yes, I am a secular priest', and then added, 'and I love that term "secular priest"'. In fact, when I was growing up, the term 'secular priest' was the commonly used expression to refer to a diocesan priest. You do not hear the term so often these days, but it is certainly an expression that highlights the fact that the diocesan priest cannot separate himself from the 'secular' world in which he lives, and the people who live in it.

I would suggest, then, that the diocesan priest finds his spirituality in the people with whom he ministers. That is the mark of the diocesan priest, and if he becomes disconnected from those people, he becomes disconnected from his spirituality. And so, while a club mentality has no place in the life of any priest, it is especially true that it has no place in the life of the diocesan priest.

Images of God

This brings me to the question of how the clergy see God. It is a crucial question, because our image of God, in many ways, influences the way we see the world around us, and the way we relate to others.

It is probably true to say that no two people have exactly the same image of God. Indeed, there would be as many images of God as there are people thinking about God.

How we see God depends as much on individual factors such as one's personality, one's family life and one's schooling, as it does on anything we learn about God, either through the Scriptures or through the Church's teaching. We process all our knowledge about God through the filter of our life story. That is why, for example, we are able to have two successive popes, Benedict and Francis, with such differing images of the same God. Pope Benedict's image is of a God who is solemn and ordered, whereas Francis' image is of a God who is far more relaxed and welcoming.

The image of God held by a particular pope, bishop, or priest is extremely important because it has an enormous influence on the thinking, and indeed the lives, of so many members of the Church. Whereas most people's image of God is an individual thing, affecting only the way they personally see God, the clergy's image of God has far more influence on the wider Church.

A good example of this is found in Pope John Paul's letter *Ordinatio Sacerdotalis*, in which he states that ordination to the priesthood is reserved to men.[7] The decision to exclude women from ordained ministry in the Church is not based on any arguments about women's ability to fulfil the role, but on the proposition that it is not what God wants. 'The Church has no authority whatsoever to confer priestly ordination on women', says the pope.[8] Presumably, God has made the decision, and so we simply have to accept it.

It is not surprising that, in the eyes of Pope John Paul II, God would not want women as part of the clergy. His image of God was not unlike that of Pope Benedict, solemn, ordered and unchanging.

At the more local level, the process is exactly the same. The parish priest who has an image of God as all-powerful and omnipotent,

---

7. Apostolic Letter *Ordinatio Sacerdotalis*, On Reserving Priestly Ordination to Men Alone, 22 May 1994, Vatican City.
8. Apostolic Letter *Ordinatio Sacerdotalis*.

stern and uncompromising, will tend to act in a similar way towards his parishioners. No matter how much he is criticised for his attitude, or encouraged to change, his image of God will override everything. 'It is not about who I am, it's about who God is'.

Of course, everyone believes that their own image of God is the correct one, although clearly, they cannot all be correct. As Christians we do have an obligation to try and verify our image of God with the reality of who the Christian God really is. We do this in many ways, but particularly by looking at the words and actions of Jesus in the Gospel. It is Jesus who ultimately is the face of God, and it is his image of God that must be the one closest to our own, whether we are members of the laity or the clergy.

Conclusion to Part 1

In this first section of the book I have described what I mean by the clergy club mentality. As I have shown, it has many dimensions, and finds its way into almost every area of the priest's life, as well as almost every area of the Church's life.

In the next section, I want to look at the origins of this clerical mentality. Where does it come from? What are the seeds of clericalism, and how do they get planted?

There must be reasons why so many members of the clergy seem to develop an attitude of superiority and exclusiveness towards the laity, while at the same time affirming that the priesthood is a ministry of service.

Part 2
Where Does the Clergy Club Mentality Come From?

Cause and Effect

Everything in society is so interrelated that it is often hard to tell which is the cause and which is the effect of any particular phenomenon. So too with clericalism. For example, in this section of the book I will be citing the Church's theology of priesthood as one of the causes of the clergy club mentality, but it is also the clergy themselves who determine and reinforce the Church's theology of priesthood. Which is the cause, and which is the effect? It is very hard to tell, and perhaps, in the final analysis, it does not really matter. What is more important is breaking the cycle that promotes the clergy club mentality, so that priests and bishops are able to develop a more welcoming and inclusive attitude towards the laity.

Also, in looking at factors that help to bring about a clerical mentality in priests, it is important to note that not all factors have the same degree of influence. Much depends on the priest himself, and on such things as his particular upbringing and parish environment. Some of these factors may have a direct influence, others may have a more indirect influence, while others may not even be relevant in a particular case. The mix is always different, but one thing is certain, and that is the fact that every young Catholic boy who goes on to become a priest is significantly influenced along the way by the Church around him, and by the clergy he encounters.

Home Environment

Many children growing up in Catholic families in the 1950s and 60s had a mixed view of their local priests. Some saw them as tough and grumpy, showing far too much emphasis on discipline and routine. Perhaps this was just a product of the era, but it certainly left its mark, and as we know only too well, many of those people still hold a negative attitude towards the clergy, perhaps even decades later.

For others though, the image of the local priest was much more positive. He was seen as someone who served his community, worked hard, was a holy man, and had the best interests of the parishioners at heart. He was given great respect, and only the best crockery was brought out when he came to visit a family home in the parish.

Certainly, for a typical young Catholic boy of the era he was someone you looked up to, and admired. He was seen as the most important person you knew, and his vocation of priesthood was described by just about everyone you knew as the best vocation you could follow.

Right from the earliest days, then, as a Catholic child, the priest was presented as someone who was different, special, and extremely important. For the boys who grew up and became priests themselves, it is not hard to see how they could easily start to see themselves in the same way, as different, special, and extremely important.

School Environment

Everybody's school experience is unique, as is their whole life journey. At the same time, however, we share a lot of common experiences with those around us, particularly with our friends, and others of similar age and background. With this in mind, I would like to say a few words about my own early years at school, not because they were particularly notable, but because I experienced the sort of things that many Catholic children of my age experienced, particularly in regard to the way the clergy, and the Church generally, had a big impact on our lives.

The priests of the parish where I grew up were a constant presence during my school years. We saw them regularly at school Masses and other liturgies. We received the sacraments of First Confession, as it was called then, and First Communion from them, and those events were very significant moments in our young lives, even if a bit nerve-wracking.

After we received our First Communion most of the boys in the class became altar servers (In those days the girls were not permitted to take on the ministry). During those years as altar servers we got to know the priests well, and while we may have been a bit scared of them at times, we always saw it as a privilege to be able to assist the priest at the altar.

Each year we would have an 'altar boys' picnic' and one particular year the parish priest took us to the archdiocesan seminary at Springwood. Although we were only in primary school at the time, the memory of that secluded location, and those young seminarians in their black soutanes, is something that I will never forget.

Another of my lasting memories of primary school is when a newly ordained priest came to the school to talk to the children. I do not remember anything of what he said, but at the end of his talk the head sister announced that we could all have the rest of the day off school, to mark this special occasion. Clearly, this young priest was a very special person if his visit to the school resulted in us being able to go home early.

All these things, and many others, were part of the Catholic culture of the day. They taught us to have great respect for the priest, and for his vocation, but in some ways also rendered him somewhat aloof and mysterious.

Seminary

Ten years after I finished primary school, in late February of 1974, I was standing on Strathfield station with a group of young men, ranging in age from seventeen to twenty-three, waiting to catch a train to Springwood. We were part of the first-year class of St Columba's College, on our way to begin studies for the diocesan priesthood. Those were the days of big numbers in the seminary. In our class alone there were thirty-four, including myself. Half of us were from the Sydney Archdiocese, the other half from various country dioceses across New South Wales. We were just ordinary guys from all sorts of different backgrounds, but within a few hours we would all be wearing black soutanes, and have clerical collars around our necks.

Everyone who has spent time in the seminary has a different story to tell. Some stories are more positive than others. For me, seminary life was challenging, but also very rewarding. It was austere and regimented, but it provided an atmosphere of reflection and learning. It took me well and truly out of my comfort zone, and helped me to grow as a person.

One thing, however, that I never really got used to, particularly in our early years at Springwood, was the isolation of seminary life. Apart from one day off a week, and an occasional afternoon doing pastoral work in the local area, the rest of the time we were expected be at the seminary, and you needed a very good excuse to get time off.

I did have one victory, however, in 1976, when I made an appointment with the seminary rector to argue my case for a couple of days' leave. As I walked into his office I had no idea how he would respond to my request. I knew I had two things in my favour. He loved music, and was a very accomplished musician. Anyway, I came straight out with it and told him that Paul McCartney and his band Wings were touring Australia and were playing a concert in Sydney, and I would give anything to be there. I would need two days off, one to get the tickets, and one to go to the concert. I don't think he had ever had a request like that before, and he said he would need a little time to think about it. When I saw him again in his office a couple of days later, the news was good. 'Alright', he said, 'you can go to the concert, but don't make a big deal about it'.

That encounter has always remained one of my treasured memories of the seminary. I do not think the rector knew much about Paul McCartney, and certainly had never heard of the band Wings. Beatle music was not to his taste. But in the atmosphere of the day it was quite a big decision, and he was certainly going out on a limb for me.

I tell that anecdote, not just because it is close to my heart, but because it also says something about the isolationist environment that so many priests grew up in, particularly in those early formative years in the seminary. And it was not just the physical environment. There was an attitude that priests were separated from the world. They didn't do normal things that other people did. There may be the occasional exception, but basically priests lived in a 'sacred' world, not a 'secular' world.

One would hope that in today's environment things are different. Indeed, if a seminarian came to the rector today, asking for permission to go to a rock concert, hopefully the rector's attitude would be something like, 'Of course you can go to the concert. Thank goodness you want to do something that so many normal young people want to do.'

Seminary life had a number of eccentricities, but one thing that always seemed a little odd was the way we had to wear priestly garb from the very first day we entered the seminary. The soutane and clerical collar was the standard required dress, except for Saturday nights, when we were able to wear ordinary clothes. I think there is something worrying about young men, some as young as seventeen, dressing as priests for the seven years of their seminary studies. It reinforces the attitude that they are different, and stand apart, right from the beginning. I remember being told once that we were not allowed to wear the clerical dress outside of the seminary grounds, on the basis that we could be seen to be impersonating a priest. If that were the case, then it is a little ironic, because that seems to be what we were doing within the seminary grounds, impersonating priests.

The role that seminary life plays in laying the seeds of clericalism is difficult to gauge, but it would be hard to argue that a culture of isolation and separation, experienced by so many priests in their formative years, has not in some way helped to bring about the disconnect between clergy and laity that is clearly evident in the Church today.

Of course, my seminary experience goes back many years, but it is a similar experience to that of many of today's priests and bishops, particularly those who currently have important leadership roles in the Church. And I suspect that while seminaries today are smaller and less regimented, some of those same attitudes are still very much present.

Integrated Personality

One of my constant concerns about the process for selecting candidates for ordination, is whether we might be accepting some men who do not demonstrate a personality that is mature and integrated.

To me, priesthood is fundamentally about leadership. Certainly, it is about many other things too. It's about holiness, service, humility, and faithfulness. But while everyone in the Church is called to be holy, to serve, to be humble and to be faithful, it is the priest, and the bishop, who are called to exercise a particular leadership role in the Church through the sacrament of Holy Orders, and to do it with both competence, and confidence.

I feel it is essential therefore, that those who are ordained to the priesthood possess the qualities of leadership. They must be mature individuals. They must be able to relate easily with people of both genders. They must have a certain degree of self-confidence. They must be able to communicate. In other words, they must be well-rounded, integrated people.

I am not saying they have to be perfect, by any stretch of the imagination. Priests and bishops will be like everyone else. They will have their strengths and weaknesses. But they must be leaders, and they must be able to demonstrate those leadership qualities before they are ordained.

It's the same for any other profession. Teachers, for example, must possess the personality and the ability to teach. They might be the nicest people in the world, but if they aren't people who can teach, they will not only be wasting their own time, but also the time of the students in the classroom.

With this in mind, I now want to look at a number of psychological and social factors that can have a bearing on one's personality and one's attitudes, to see what role they might play in helping to form a clerical mind set, and indeed, to see whether, in these factors, we may discover the seeds of a club mentality.

The Need to be Accepted

We all want to be accepted. It is just part of the human condition. We particularly want to be accepted by our peers, and by the significant people in our lives.

Priests are no different. Indeed, perhaps because they don't have wives and children, there is a greater need among priests to be accepted by their colleagues, and particularly by their bishop. Maybe this is even more the case for diocesan priests, who do not have the support of a religious community.

In any case, it is clear that priests like to be recognised and appreciated, and they certainly value affirmation and praise, particularly when it comes from the bishop.

In a similar way, they understandably feel unappreciated if that recognition and affirmation is not forthcoming, as is evidenced by a remark made by one senior Sydney priest who said that in all his years ministering in the archdiocese, he had never once been asked for his advice on anything.

I think many priests can relate to that sentiment.

With regard to the desire to be recognised and affirmed, which, as I say, is a very normal thing, the problem arises when the priest actually depends on that affirmation for his own sense of self-worth and self-confidence, rather than having an inherent, healthy self-image.

I firmly believe that many, if not most, of the problems that arise in relationships have their origin in a lack of self-esteem and self-confidence. When people do not feel good about themselves, it is difficult for them to develop positive relationships with others. This is crucial for the diocesan priest, who has to relate to so many people in so many different circumstances.

Firstly, priests themselves have to be able to relate to each other. They have to be able to work together, and often live together, in a positive and productive way. Thankfully, there are many situations where this does happen, but it is not always the case.

Many priests have heard horror stories from colleagues who have had to live in very difficult presbytery situations. I know, too, from my time on the committee that looked at priests' appointments, the overriding factor determining a particular appointment was not the needs of the parish, but whether the parish priest was difficult, or easy, to get on with.

The diocesan priest also has to develop a good working relationship with the parish staff. If there are horror stories from priests living with other priests in presbyteries, there are also horror stories from secretaries and pastoral workers trying to work with priests, in what are sometimes very difficult and stressful parish situations.

Then, of course, the priest has to relate to hundreds, sometimes thousands of parishioners and visitors to the parish, and here again, we know that he does not always do this well. Sadly, there have been too many instances of priests being dismissive and ill-mannered towards their parishioners, and at times, almost going out of their way to make life difficult for the people they are supposed to be serving.

There are a number of reasons why this might happen, I am sure, but I would suggest that in many cases, at least one of the contributing factors is the priest's, or bishop's, lack of self-esteem. Any little thing that goes wrong, or is not to his liking, puts him immediately on the defensive. He reacts, rather than responds. He feels threatened, and uses his power and position to get his way, rather than being able to listen, and discuss the issue in a mature way.

It is therefore most important that the issue of self-esteem is addressed from the time the seminarian first begins his training. We probably all suffer a little from a lack of self-confidence - that's just normal. But if there is a serious issue in this regard with someone who is studying for the priesthood, then it cannot be ignored. Everything must be done to help the seminarian recognise his true worth, and to ensure that, as a priest, he does not use inappropriate behaviour as a way to bolster his self-esteem.

Finally, I want to make an observation in relation to the bishop's responsibility to affirm and encourage the priests of the diocese.

I know that giving someone affirmation is not always an easy thing to do, particularly if it is to one of your professional colleagues. I know also, that bishops really do try to find ways to recognise and show appreciation for their priests, through correspondence from the chancery, or cards sent out to the priests at the time of their ordination anniversaries. But they are always form letters, or standard cards with the appropriate name typed in. I recognise that there are time restrictions on everyone, but I do believe that something like a two-minute phone call by the archbishop, to each priest in the archdiocese, even if it were only once every ten years, just to say hello, would do far more good, for both the priest and the archbishop, than all the words that come from the chancery in formal correspondence.

The Need for Security and Safety

One day at a parish where I was appointed, we were hosting the local deanery meeting, a formal gathering of the priests of the area, followed by lunch. For this particular meeting we had invited two people from one of the social service agencies in the archdiocese to speak to us about their work. Two women came to represent the agency. They arrived early, and set up their presentation in one of the large meeting rooms in the presbytery, and awaited the arrival of the priests.

As the twenty-or-so priests filed into the room I was struck by how little attention they gave to the two guests. Some gave a cursory glance, or a quick hello, as they went past. Some headed straight to a group of priests who had already arrived, without even acknowledging the two women. Others gave an awkward smile. Finally, one stopped and introduced himself, and then one or two others joined him.

I have seen this phenomenon many times over the years, priests gravitating towards each other, rather than engaging with the laity. Of course, we all feel more comfortable with those we know. None of us likes moving into unfamiliar territory. But among priests, the gravitational pull of the clergy club is very strong. In the club the priest is safe and secure. No one is going to challenge him. No one is going to ask him any difficult questions. No one is going to move him out of his comfort zone.

Clerical Dress

The question of what a priest wears often comes up in discussions about clericalism. Personally, it is not an issue that I feel strongly about. I am much more interested in the way priests relate, particularly with the laity.

However, having said that, the issue is certainly worthy of discussion, as it does say something about attitudes and perceptions.

It is the case in the Sydney Archdiocese that priests are able to choose to dress as they wish. Some wear full clerical dress, with black suit and collar. Some wear no form of clerical dress at all. Some wear something in the middle, perhaps a white shirt and a cross. Of course, as for anyone, the choice of dress will depend on the occasion and the setting, but in general, most priests will tend towards one of the three options mentioned above, depending on, among other things, their personality and their theology.

I, personally, have chosen not to wear any form of clerical dress, which incidentally, was for centuries, the traditional custom for diocesan priests, as distinct from religious order priests, who wore the dress of their order. I have made this decision, simply because it is another way that I feel more connected to the laity, or perhaps I should say, less disconnected from the laity.

I know some priests wear clerical dress so that when they are in public, people will know who they are, and so that those who wish to, will be able to engage in conversation with them. I perfectly understand this argument, and ultimately it will always come down to a personal choice.

Clerical Titles

The question of whether a priest wishes to be addressed by a title, rather than by name, is another contentious issue, and is often related to that of clerical dress. I know that some priests feel the title 'Father' is a beautiful title, and says so much about the pastoral relationship between the priest and the laity. There is certainly truth in this argument, but ultimately a title is a title, and always suggests an imbalance in the relationship. I feel it is difficult for two people to have a worthwhile relationship with each other, if one, and only one, is being addressed by a title. It is clearly not a relationship of equals, and that is not a good start for any relationship.

In my own case, if people address me as 'Father', and some people insist on doing so, I don't make a fuss about it, but I must admit I do feel uncomfortable having the people I am supposed to serve, addressing me by a title.

I know there is an argument that the title is being used to show respect for the priesthood, as much as for the priest himself, and once again I understand that position, but surely, respect ultimately has nothing to do with titles. In fact, if we think about it, the people we respect most are more likely to be the people with whom we are on first name terms.

A Lay Perspective

From the perspective of the laity, the use of both titles and clerical dress is perceived in different ways. Some people see a priest wanting to be addressed as 'Father', as a bit pompous, while others will see it as the appropriate thing to do. In a similar way, some will see the wearing of clerical dress as an attempt by the priest to be noticed, while others will see it as a witness to the priesthood, and to the Church.

I even had one personal experience where the messages from a layperson were quite mixed. There was an elderly gentleman in the parish, a wonderful man, who had not seen me in clerical clothes all the time I had been at the parish, until we met one day, both attending the same funeral. I had decided to wear a clerical shirt and collar to the funeral, and when he saw me, he looked twice, and said, 'Aren't you one of us anymore?'

That same man insisted on calling me 'Father', rather than using my name. He was uncomfortable with clerical dress, but very comfortable with the clerical title.

Ultimately, as priests, we simply have to make sure that any decisions we end up making about clerical dress and titles, are not coming from a desire to see ourselves as more important than the laity, just as bishops have to make sure that any decisions they make about dress and titles are not coming from any desire to see themselves as more important than the priests.

It is a question that never goes away, because, as a priest, whenever you meet people in a new setting, they are never quite sure how to address you, and you have to give them a lead. My own response is to say that I prefer to be called "John," but I am happy with whatever they are comfortable with.

Insular Mentality

The life of a priest or bishop, by its very nature, tends to have an insular dimension to it. As clergy, we don't have the same life experiences that most people have. We do not have our own families, and so do not experience the joys and challenges of family life. Our work colleagues at the leadership level are all male, and so we don't experience the dynamic of working with both genders in such areas as professional development and ongoing education. Even at the practical day-to-day level, we don't experience the normal financial pressures that others do. Everything is provided for us—the house, the car, food, electricity, cleaning, and more. In the parish we are often shielded from the truth, particularly if the parishioners think it is something that Father won't want to hear. One could also add that we tend to live in a very Catholic world. We work almost exclusively in a Catholic environment, and for many of us, our friends and acquaintances are mostly Catholic.

This does not mean, of course, that the clergy cannot live full and integrated lives, but it does require constant awareness on the part of priests and bishops, that the way they see the world is not the way most people see the world. The clerical view is often narrower, more simplistic, and sometimes very black and white. This can result in priests being uncomfortable interacting with a whole cross-section of society, and particularly with those who hold views different to their own.

Some years ago, at one of our clergy conferences, we had a guest speaker who gave a talk on atheism. He had prepared well and delivered a good talk. The only problem was he was a Catholic, and with the best of intentions, could only speak about atheism from a Catholic perspective.

I made the comment in discussion after the talk, that it would have been good to hear a talk on atheism, given by an atheist, but my words fell on deaf ears. It was obvious that having someone speak to the clergy from a non-religious perspective was always going to be a bridge too far.

Of course, I can understand why the bishops would be reluctant to invite an atheist to speak to a group of priests. No one likes giving a platform to views that are completely opposed to your own, or to be seen to be encouraging a different viewpoint. But both as individual priests, and as a hierarchy, we must make sure that we don't allow our insular perspective on the world to cut us off from those who are also genuinely searching for meaning and truth in life. Otherwise we can end up with, not only an insular mentality, but a siege mentality, where we start to think that everyone is against us, everyone that is, who does not follow traditional Catholic teaching.

An insular mentality will also stifle personal growth, and hinder the development of one's full potential. A priest who lives in an insular world will not mature as a fully integrated human being. He is shielded from the normal demands of life that challenge everyone to be the best person they can be. In a similar way, the laity will not grow as mature Catholics if they are not allowed to interact with the clergy in an adult way, but are always kept on the sidelines, out of the discussions, and out of the decision-making process.

Models of Church

If you ask the question, 'Who is the head of the Church?' you will probably get one of two answers—the pope, or Jesus. Both answers are correct, depending on the context of the discussion. When the question is asked without any particular context, it is then up to the responder to provide his or her own context, and the result will usually be one or other of the two answers. Those who say the Pope is the head of the Church are coming from a top-down, hierarchical model of Church, while those who say Jesus is the head of the Church are coming from a broader, more scriptural model.

There are many different models of Church. In 1974 a groundbreaking book entitled 'Models of Church' was published, in which the author, Jesuit priest Avery Dulles, described six different models of Church, as diverse as the institutional model and the servant model.[1]

---

1. Avery Dulles, *Models of Church* (Crown Publishing Group, 2002).

There is no particular model that is more correct than the others. They all have something to say about the complex community we call Church. In terms of the clergy club mentality, however, it is clear that some models support a more clerical view of the Church, while other models work against it. The institutional model focusses on the structure, authority and constancy of the Church, and thus works to reinforce a clerical mentality. On the other hand, the servant model centres on the Church as the people of God, who have been called to establish Christ's kingship of peace, justice and love in the world. Clearly, the servant model does not fit so easily with a clergy club mentality.

It is not surprising that the majority of priests who become bishops work out of an institutional model of Church. The hierarchy promotes those members of the clergy who have a similar mind set to themselves, who will reinforce the structures and culture of the Church, and keep things as they are. That is not to say that priests with a more people-orientated model of Church are never appointed as bishops. It is just that they are rarely promoted to positions of greater responsibility.

The big exception to the rule, however, is Pope Francis. It is indeed one of the mysteries of the modern Church how Jorge Mario Bergoglio was elected as the 266th Pope. His model of Church is anything but institutional, and he has brought a refreshingly new and inclusive approach to the papacy. One can only assume that after decades of the dour reigns of Pope John Paul II and Pope Benedict, even the cardinals were looking for a change.

Passing on the Faith

One of the duties that the bishops take very seriously, and rightly so, is the responsibility to protect, and pass on, the body of Catholic faith. The Catholic Church is an apostolic Church, founded on Jesus, and has a rich tradition that must be respected and maintained. I feel, however, that the hierarchy's view of the Church's ongoing tradition, and their role in it, is perceived in a way that is too static and linear, always looking back at the past, rather than taking the messages of the past and applying them to the present day.

Sometimes when I hear bishops talking about the passing on of the faith it reminds me of what I call the 'football' model of tradition. The faith was given to the apostles by Jesus, the Holy Spirit confirmed that faith in them at Pentecost, and then they passed it on, through the bishops, from one generation to the next, each one ensuring that nothing happened to it on the way, with the next bishop receiving it in the exact same form as it had been received by the previous one.

I once heard a bishop who had come to the parish to speak to children who were preparing for Confirmation, telling the children how he had been ordained by another bishop, who himself had been ordained by another bishop, and so on, and if you went back far enough you would get back to one of the apostles, and, in fact, he wondered which one of the apostles was at the beginning of the line for him.

I am not being critical of the bishop's talk. He was speaking to young children, and he was trying to help them understand the richness of the Church's tradition. But our faith is not dependent on a linear progression from the apostles. Yes, the Holy Spirit came upon the apostles in the first century, at Pentecost, but that same Spirit came upon the Church in the second century, and the third, and comes upon the Church today, the very same Spirit, with the same gifts, and the same grace. When we celebrate the feast of Pentecost today, we are doing far more than remembering what took place 2,000 years ago. It is our Pentecost, just as real, just as powerful, and just as efficacious as the Pentecost the apostles experienced in Jerusalem. The Holy Spirit is not passed on through history by the bishops. It 'blows where it chooses' (Jn3:8).

The way the hierarchy sees the Holy Spirt working in the Church, and the way they see their own role, in terms of 'passing on' the faith, has an enormous effect on how the Church works in the modern world. The 'football' model is safe and secure. All the decisions have been made, back in the first century, and the role of the Church is simply to maintain the status quo, perhaps tweaking it a little here and there. A more dynamic, contemporary model, however, challenges the Church to live in the modern world, to interpret faith in a way that incorporates development and change, and to accept the fact that the hierarchy today has the authority to make decisions that may not necessarily be the same as those the hierarchy of the early Church made, or would have made, in a very different era.

It is not surprising that the current Church hierarchy tend to use a linear model of faith and tradition, always going back to the past in order to find answers to contemporary questions. This model reinforces traditional views, makes change difficult, and in the process, strengthens the clergy club mentality.

Theology of Priesthood

In our years in the seminary we often heard the expression that the priest is 'in the world, but not of the world'. The idea is that the priest, while obviously living in the same world as everyone else, was not connected to the world in the same way as everyone else. He was 'otherworldly', rather than 'worldly'. He was 'sacred', rather than 'secular'.

Of course, there are many interpretations of this expression, but it does imply that holiness is not found in the physical creation around us, but in the spiritual world, that we cannot see.

I appreciate what the expression is saying, and I certainly don't wish to trivialise the sentiment behind it. We all find ultimate meaning in the spiritual, even if that meaning has its source in the physical.

The problem with the notion, however, in the context of the clergy club, is that it pushes the idea that priests are essentially different from other people, and special. They belong to the spiritual world in a way that others do not.

This idea is reinforced by the theology of ontological change, which states that, through the sacrament of Holy Orders, priests and bishops are changed, in their very being, when they are ordained. The priest is seen as intrinsically different to the layperson at a very fundamental level.

The theology of ontological change in priests, through ordination, is still the official, current thinking on priesthood in the Church. Sometimes you see subtle expressions of the notion coming through in Church literature. For some years I received a journal with the title *Priests and People*.[2] It is a rather odd title when you think about it, as priests are obviously people too, but the distinction between those who are ordained in the Church, and those who are not ordained, is so much part of the Catholic mentality that the phrase 'priests and people' can almost go unnoticed. In fact, I had been familiar with the journal for years and saw nothing unusual in the title until one day a friend, who is not in the club, pointed it out to me.

The argument that priests have been changed ontologically through ordination is clearly very hard to support on philosophical grounds, and I am not sure how far the bishops would try to push it in

---

2. The journal *Priests and People* began in 1931 under the title *The Clergy Review*. In 1987 it was re-named *Priests and People* and in 2004 it was again re-titled as *The Pastoral Review*. It is published by Tablet Publishing.

any rational debate on the issue. But for the clergy it is a very power-ful psychological factor in determining how they see themselves, and particularly how they see themselves in relation to the laity. In some ways, it lies at the very heart of the whole concept of the clergy club mentality.

The Nature of Institutions

It is sometimes said that all institutions, whether they be a private company, a government agency, an international fund-raising organ-isation, or the local golf club, start off with the best of intentions, and a sincere desire to work for the benefit of those for whom the institu-tion was set up, but somewhere along the line the primary motivation becomes maintaining and protecting the institution itself.

It may seem a rather cynical observation, but there is a lot of truth in the statement. When people of like mind come together to form any sort of association, they invest a lot of energy, and a lot of them-selves, into the new entity. They develop a great sense of belonging to the association, and in some cases, may even get to the stage where they cannot imagine living without it.

It is not hard to see then, how the need arises to maintain the institution's existence, and to protect the institution whenever that existence, or its reputation, is in danger. Churches in particular, are good examples of this phenomenon, perhaps because their members have invested so much of themselves in the institution. It could be argued that in the Catholic Church it is the clergy who have invested the most, at a personal level, and so they are the ones who are most protective of the institution.

It is when the Church is being criticised or comes under threat in some way, that the clergy close ranks, and the club mentality is most evident. I remember being at a dinner one night with a group of people, including a number of priests and a bishop. At the time, Pope Benedict had just made some comments about Islam which had caused quite a bit of controversy, particularly among the Muslim community. We were discussing the Pope's comments and someone asked the bishop whether he agreed with what Pope Benedict had said. The bishop's reply was, 'I would always support the Pope'. In other words, whatever the Pope says should never be questioned.

The Hierarchical Problem

The Catholic Church would be among the most hierarchical institutions in the world. Ultimately all power is invested in one person at the top, the pope. He is elected by the next group in the hierarchy, the cardinals. Then come the bishops, the priests and finally the laity. Everyone knows their place, and nobody can act outside their particular grouping.

The hierarchical structure certainly has its advantages. It keeps the institution ordered, and tightly bound. It also ensures a consistency in beliefs and practices. One of the great strengths of the Catholic Church is that you know exactly what it teaches, and its teachings are universal. You know exactly where you stand.

But the hierarchical nature of the Church also has a serious disadvantage. It breeds a hierarchical mentality, particularly in the clergy. Consciously or unconsciously, attitudes develop towards others in the Church that are based on position and rank. And given that the laity hold the lowest position, and the bottom rank, it is not surprising that a club mentality could develop among the clergy. The seeds are there in every aspect of the Church's structure.

It is interesting to note that whenever the various groupings of people in the Church are mentioned, whether in papal documents or in less formal correspondence, they are always listed in strict order, from the pope down to the laity. Even in the eucharistic prayers of the Mass, the ranking of Church members holds fast. We pray for the pope, bishops, priests, deacons, and finally the laity. The wording is not always the same in each eucharistic prayer, but one thing is consistent, the laity are always last.

The Secular/Sacred Distinction

When I was appointed to my first parish as parish priest, even before I took up the appointment, I went over to the parish and made a visit to the church. I had not been inside that particular church before. It was a beautiful old church, but there was one thing that struck me immediately, and that was the altar rails. They were made of imitation marble, and virtually cut the church in two, dividing the priest's side from the congregation's side.

That was certainly not my model of Church, and I wondered whether, at some point, we as a parish, might be able to have a look at the issue. I didn't do anything for at least six months or so, but then I decided to raise the matter with the parish community. One Sunday at the Masses I spoke about the altar rails, and how their purpose was to divide the sacred area of the church, which was reserved for the clergy, from the rest of the church. I said how I felt they were a barrier, dividing me from the congregation, and in any case, the whole church was sacred. I invited them to talk to me about their feelings on the issue.

The response was overwhelmingly in favour of removing the altar rails, and we completed the job shortly after. At the practical level, we were then able to open up the church, and make it far more liturgically friendly. The children, in particular, were now able to be much more involved, at both Sunday Masses and school Masses. But more importantly, a statement had been made that we were going to be one community, clergy and laity together, celebrating our faith, without anything coming between us.

The secular/sacred distinction is, I believe, one of the driving forces behind the clergy club mentality. It immediately sets up two classes of Catholics—the sacred clergy and the secular laity. When you have this situation, it is not hard to see how the clergy come to see themselves as closer to God than the laity, and in the same way, it is not hard to see how the laity come to see themselves as inferior to the clergy, unable to share in their sacred, holy status. In reality of course, holiness has nothing to do with whether one is a priest, bishop, schoolteacher, or builder, but everything to do with what is in your heart, and how you act on it.

Mystique of the Priesthood

One night, after a parish council meeting, a few of us were sitting around having a drink, and solving the problems of the world, when the conversation turned to the topic of heaven and the after-life. In the course of the discussion I made the remark, 'I certainly hope there is a heaven'.

At that point one of the council members said to me, 'You're a priest, how can you say you hope there is a heaven. You must know there is a heaven'.

I responded that I was like everyone else. I had no special knowledge about heaven, or about God, or about the after-life. I lived in hope, and faith, believing that the words of Jesus are true.

Many people think that the priest has some sort of special connection to God. It's part of the mystique of the priesthood. People constantly ask me to pray for particular intentions, and of course, I do. But their own prayers are just as efficacious as the prayers of the priest.

It's not hard to understand how a mystique has grown up around the priesthood, particularly among the Catholic laity. In Church theology, the priest is described as acting '*in persona Christi*', that is, in the person of Christ. There is a very real sense in which all Christians act in the person of Christ, but the Church's theology is not saying that. Rather, it is saying that the priest is acting in the person of Christ in a way that the laity cannot. It is just another way of saying that the priest is more like Christ than the laity will ever be. Of course this is not true, but the mystique continues, and is reinforced by Church doctrine and Church liturgy.

One particular way that the mystique is carried on is through the use of Latin in the liturgy. Certainly, there are some Catholics who hanker for the pre-Vatican Church, and the Latin Mass, but they are few in number. Most of the enthusiasm for the use of Latin in the liturgy comes from the clergy, and understandably so, as it is the language of the clergy, or at least it was in the past. As more and more priests say Mass in Latin, more and more of the laity, who have little or no knowledge of the language, will become further disempowered, and in the process, the mystique of the priesthood will grow.

Another aspect of priesthood that reinforces this mystique is the rule of compulsory celibacy, which operates in the Latin rite. The idea of someone promising never to marry, for religious reasons, fascinates many people. Often, when I am at a social gathering and someone asks me what I do as a job, and I tell them I am a Catholic priest, I get a response something like, 'You are the ones who can't marry, aren't you?' It is the first thing that people think of, and in many cases the one thing they want to talk about. While it is certainly good that people want to engage in a discussion about the priesthood, I always feel that their interest is motivated by what they see as a mysterious and curious life-style, rather than by a genuine concern for religion and faith.

A Male Club

There is a story told about a bishop who was once talking to a group of children at a school assembly. He wanted to find out what they knew about the Church, so he asked them the question, 'How many sacraments are there?' After a short pause, one young girl put her hand up and said, 'Seven for boys, and six for girls'.

In her answer to the bishop's question that young girl highlighted an issue that simply won't go away for the Church hierarchy, 'Should women continue to be excluded from full participation in the life of the Catholic Church?' 'Should they not be able to receive all seven sacraments?'

Certainly, progress has been made over the last fifty years in regard to women being able to participate more fully in the life of the Church. The ban on girls serving at the altar has been lifted, and women are now able to act as readers and acolytes, even if they are not able to be formally instituted into the ministries, as men are. I live in hope that one day, women will be able to participate in all ministries in the Church, and to be able to receive all seven of the sacraments.

But my purpose in this book is not to argue why women should be welcomed into full participation in the life of the Church. This book is about the clergy club, and I want to say something about how the exclusion of women from the club affects how the club thinks and operates.

The most obvious deficiency of an all-male clergy is that priests and bishops have very little interaction with women at a professional level, and thus there is no moderating effect of women's strengths, particularly in areas where men might struggle. An example of this can be seen when looking at the current issue of clergy abuse of children.

It has been asserted many times in the debate, and I believe correctly so, that the child sexual abuse scandal would never have got to the stage it has, if women had been on the committees deciding whether or not to send on to other parishes those priests who were suspected of committing crimes against children. The argument is that women have a greater sensitivity to the needs of children, and a greater sense of protection of children, especially the most vulnerable. It is too late now to change what has happened, but hopefully the bishops will be able to see their way clear to accept women on to committees that deal with the placement of priests, and to include them in discussions and decision-making regarding these appointments. Surely the need to protect vulnerable children should override the bishops' desire to have clergy-only committees in these areas. And, in any case, even apart from the issue of safeguarding children, having women on these committees with the appropriate skills and training, would bring a dimension to the discussions that is currently lacking.

The attitude of priests and bishops towards women is always an important part of the discussion on clericalism. Many priests have had little or no contact with women at a professional level, and find it difficult working with them in that context. In particular, some priests from overseas, especially those from countries where women are still battling for recognition, have been unable to accept situations such as the principal of the local Catholic school often being a woman, and having all the authority that comes with the position.

The hierarchy's attitude towards women can be seen in many ways. In 1993, when I was doing some post-graduate studies in Rome, I attended a Mass in the Vatican that was celebrated by Pope John Paul II. It was a small group of Australians who had gathered for the Mass in the Pope's private chapel, and when it had finished, I noticed that the Pope was taking off his chasuble, and his other vestments, while he remained on the sanctuary. He had an assistant with him who took each of the vestments one by one, and then dropped them unceremoniously into the arms of a nun standing by, who was dutifully catching each one as it arrived. It was around the time that Pope John Paul published his statement on the ordination of women, and I realised from the attitude that was displayed towards this woman, why the Pope, even with the best of intentions, could not see how women could ever participate at any decision-making level in the Church.

Even Pope Francis seems to be caught up in 1950s stereotypes of women. When Donald and Melania Trump visited him at the Vatican in 2017, after speaking with the President, Pope Francis then turned and spoke to Melania, asking her 'What are you feeding him, potica?'[3] No serious questions for the woman. Only references to cooking, and looking after her husband. Perhaps this explains Pope Francis' less than enthusiastic comments regarding women's participation in leadership roles in the Church.

---

3. Potica is a bread or cake with a rich filling, including nuts. It is an East European cuisine.

Advocacy

One of the things that has always puzzled me regarding the position of women in the Church, is why so few priests or bishops ever advocate on their behalf. Because of the structure of the Catholic Church, change can only take place from the top down, so if women are ever going to be able to participate more fully in the Church, the initiative, and certainly the decision, must come from the clergy.

Yet priests and bishops are extremely reticent to raise the topic. Even those among the clergy who I know are in favour of women being more involved in the life of the Church, do not wish to discuss the matter, at least in any sort of public forum. Often the comment is made that there are other more pressing issues for the bishops to address. When I raise the issue, for example, of why the institution of readers and acolytes, which are lay ministries, is still restricted to men, I always seem to get an answer like, 'Women have been given permission to do what readers and acolytes do, they are just not able to be instituted, or to use the terms "reader" or "acolyte." What's the problem?'

Clearly there is a problem, and it needs to be addressed. With a clergy club mentality, however, even a straightforward issue like not excluding women from lay ministry, is a long way from being resolved.

A Celibate Club

I have a friend who is a Ukrainian rite Catholic priest. One day he called me, just as I was getting ready to go to one of the aged care facilities in the parish to celebrate Mass. He said he was in the area and if I was free, he would drop in and say hello. I asked if he would like to come with me to celebrate Mass, and then we could catch up after that. He agreed, and that is exactly what we did.

At the Mass the regular group had assembled around the makeshift altar, and I asked my friend if he would like to be the main celebrant, which he was pleased to do. When Mass was over I invited him to say a few words to the congregation about his story. When he explained that he was married, with two children, some of the people nearly fell off their chairs. Most of them had never seen a married Catholic priest, let alone have one celebrate Mass with them.

It is hard for a typical Catholic in the Latin rite to imagine a Church with married priests. Some think of Anglican ministers who are married, and assume it would be sort of like that, substituting the Catholic priest for the Anglican minister. Others think of the celibate model they know, then add in a wife and children. Neither scenario would adequately describe what a married Latin rite Catholic priesthood might look like.

Of course, it is not easy to imagine something you have never seen, but that should not be a barrier to opening up the question, and looking at the possibilities.

Sadly, it is virtually impossible to get bishops to even discuss questions around celibacy, and whether it should be compulsory or optional in the Latin rite. Perhaps this in itself gives an insight into how significant the policy of compulsory celibacy is, in reinforcing the clergy club mentality.

Celibacy and Club Loyalty

The fact that priests and bishops are celibate means that they are not personally involved with some of the moral issues regarding marriage and family, which the Church hierarchy has traditionally taken a hard line on. These issues, such as contraception and divorce, are looked at from a theoretical perspective only, by those who are making the decisions. If, however, the clergy themselves had to deal with these issues in their own lives, there could well be a loosening of the hardline position, let us say on contraception, as the priests experience the reality that day-to-day life is more complex and problematic than the natural law theory on which the contraception ban is based.

It is not, however, only issues such as contraception and divorce that are removed from the real-life experience of the celibate clergy. Being married and having a family brings with it a new perspective on a whole range of issues, particularly because of the extra responsibility and concern that comes with having a spouse and children.

Let us take, for example, the Church's ban on gluten-free altar breads.[4] While some people who suffer from coeliac disease are able to tolerate a small amount of gluten, and so are able to receive

---

4. Later in the book I will go into more detail about gluten-free bread and the Church's ban on its use for Holy Communion.

low-gluten altar breads, there are others who cannot tolerate any gluten at all. These are the people who are unable to receive the host at Mass, as currently all communion breads must be made from wheat, and gluten is a protein that is found naturally in all wheat products.

For the celibate priest, the only way that he is affected personally by this ruling is if he himself suffers from a severe gluten allergy. If priests were married with a family, however, it may well be the case that one of his children, let's say his daughter, has coeliac disease, and thus is unable to make her First Communion, or indeed receive Communion at all. Now, the gluten-free argument moves from a theological construct to something very real and personal, as the priest tries to explain to his eight-year-old daughter why she is not able to receive Holy Communion like everyone else.

Suddenly, for the priest, loyalty to the Church's ruling is challenged by love for his child, and it is not hard to see how he may be tempted to use a gluten-free altar bread to allow his daughter to receive Holy Communion, whereas before it would never have been an issue.

Celibacy, Logistics and Cost

One of the reasons why any sort of change in the celibacy rule will be difficult to achieve, or indeed, why any sort of discussion on the topic is difficult to initiate, is because the clergy, who have taken on celibacy themselves, are comfortable, one would imagine, with their decision and with their celibate lifestyles, and see no reason to change the status quo. There is a need in all of us to justify our position on things, particularly big, lifestyle decisions. A priest who says that he would be just as good and effective a priest, even if he were married, is at least implicitly, questioning the need for compulsory celibacy, and thus his own decision to take the vow.

Another reason why bishops in particular might be slow to engage in a discussion on compulsory celibacy is that, having priests unmarried, certainly makes it easier for the bishops to move priests to different parishes, or even to send them further afield, such as overseas for post-graduate studies.

For example, to move a priest to a new parish is, under the current system, a simple operation. The priest is formally appointed to his new assignment, packs up his belongings, says his goodbyes, and is ready to start at the new parish with very short notice. If he were married, however, it would be a far more complicated procedure. Such things as the children's schools, the working arrangements of the priest's wife, and other family commitments would have to be taken into consideration. Of course, these issues are not insurmountable, and are dealt with successfully in many other professions, but it would certainly be an added reason why bishops would be reluctant to change the status quo.

Another practical issue helping to perpetuate the celibate model of priesthood is the economic factor. Clearly, supporting a single priest is far less expensive than supporting both the priest and his family. In some of the bigger parishes there are sometimes two or three priests living and ministering together in the one parish community. Under the current system, with the priests living in the same presbytery, it is a very cost-effective arrangement. Obviously, this situation would need to change if the priests were married, as each priest would then require his own family home. This, of course, would result in the combined costs of the new living arrangements being much higher.

One would like to think that the Church's decisions about priestly celibacy were not made on an economic basis, but as in all areas of life, it is a factor that cannot be ignored, and would certainly contribute towards maintaining the clergy club as a celibate group.

As a final observation on the celibate model of priesthood, I just want to make a comment on the laity's perspective on compulsory celibacy, at least as I see it.

It seems to me that parishioners are more interested in who their parish priest actually is, rather than whether he is married or single. In every parish that I have been in, I have asked parishioners the question, 'Would you still want me as your priest, if I were married?' The response has been overwhelmingly, 'Yes'. I do not think they responded that way just to be kind, or not wishing to offend me. The laity simply want to have a priest they can get on with, and work with, whatever his marital status. It is the clergy who are more concerned with maintaining the celibate model.

Historical Perspective

The clergy club mentality is not just a social, or psychological, or theological phenomenon. It also has an historical dimension. The disconnection between those who are ordained, and those who are not ordained, is not a modern occurrence, but has its roots in the Church's long and, at times, tumultuous history.

I just want to look very briefly at one particular period in that history which had a huge effect on the way the Church hierarchy saw themselves in relation to the rest of society, and which I believe still permeates much of the thinking of the clergy today. It is the period from the mid-1800s to the early part of the 20ᵗʰ century.

This period was a very difficult time in the Church's history. Life was changing rapidly, and the Church was struggling to come to terms with a world that was no longer grounded in the medieval and religious structures of the past, but which was moving into a new era, characterised by individualism and science, rather than tradition and religion.

The tension between the thinking of the Church hierarchy on the one hand, and the views of contemporary society on the other, can be seen in the writings of Pope Pius IX, who was Pope from 1846 to 1878. In his document *The Syllabus of Errors*[5] promulgated in 1864, Pope Pius lists 80 statements that sum up various aspects of the thinking of his day, and then declares each one of them to be an error. He criticises such things as freedom of the press, freedom to practise religions other than the Catholic religion, and the separation of Church and State. But perhaps it is the following statement that best sums up the Pope's perspective on the world, when he says that it is an error to believe that 'The Roman Pontiff can, and ought to, reconcile himself, and come to terms with progress, liberalism and modern civilisation.'[6]

Of course, any papal statement must be read in its historical context, and clearly the Pope was defending what he saw as an attack on the Church and its teachings, but the hierarchy's struggle to come to terms with 'progress, liberalism and modern civilisation' continues today. Indeed, the Church hierarchy still views the world from a deductive, natural law perspective, while so many others view it from a more empirical, rational perspective. It is no wonder that religion and science seem to be having more and more difficulty finding any sort of common ground.

---

5. The Syllabus of Errors was promulgated by Pope Pius 1X on 9 June 1864. See 'Papal Encyclicals Online'.
6. The Syllabus of Errors, statement 80.

A particular question facing the Church at the time of Pope Pius IX was the issue of democracy. The idea that authority came from the people, rather than from the rulers, had been around, of course, for a long time, but it was only in the post French Revolution period that it really took hold, and started to become a reality, at least in the Western world. This notion of democracy, where people could choose their leaders, went directly against the Church's model of authority, where leaders were chosen by the hierarchy, and authority was given to them by God.

The Catholic Church, of course, accepts democracy as a reality in the world, at least in the secular arena, but the traditional Church mentality, that power comes from the top, runs deep in the clergy culture. I believe that the inability of many priests and bishops to encourage lay ministry, particularly in the area of decision-making, goes back to this question of authority, and where it comes from. It is very difficult for many clergy to really believe that someone who is not ordained, could actually share in the exercise of the Church's authority.

Conclusion to Part 2

In this section I have looked at the origins of clericalism, and reflected on the various ways a club mentality can develop among the clergy. In the next part I will be looking at how this mentality expresses itself in the day-to-day lives of the clergy, and just as importantly, how the club mentality is reinforced by the Church structures.

Part 3
How does the Clergy Club Mentality Express Itself?

The Messiah Complex

The first fervour of priestly ministry is a very powerful experience. I remember, in my own case, going off to my first parish, ready to change the world, and to save the world. I had completed seven years of full time study, including courses on various branches of theology, philosophy and the Scriptures. I had also spent an enormous amount of time in prayer, meditation, and spiritual reflection. I was an *Alter Christus*, another Christ, and the time had now come for me to begin my ministry.

It was just a few weeks after ordination when I had my first reality check. I was celebrating Sunday Mass, reflecting on the profound mystery of the Eucharist, when I noticed an elderly gentleman, kneeling in one of the front pews, saying the rosary. I remember thinking to myself, 'Fancy saying the rosary during Mass. The Mass is the high point of the Church's liturgy'.

As I looked again, I was struck by the man's large, wrinkled hands, resting on the top of the pew, and his craggy face bowed in prayer. The rosary beads were dangling from his hands, as they had clearly done countless times before. My irritation at the situation was quickly turning to admiration and respect, and an overriding sense that this man's prayer was every bit as important as the Mass that was being celebrated, and certainly that day, far worthier than my own distracted thoughts.

It is difficult for a newly ordained priest not to have some feeling that 'I am here to teach you, to strengthen your faith, to show you who God is'. That's what priests are supposed to do.

The only problem is, many of the parishioners have a more profound spirituality, a deeper faith, and a wider life experience than the
newly ordained priest. I soon came to realise that instead of me teaching the parishioners, we would be teaching each other, instead of me
strengthening their faith, we would be strengthening each other's
faith, and instead of me showing them who God is, we would be,
together, discovering God in our midst, and in each other.

Unfortunately, it is not always easy for the clergy to recognise this
reality, and to put it into practice on a consistent basis. We are so
imbued with the idea that, as priests, we 'save souls'. That very expression implies that the priest's soul is saved, and he will do his best to
save the souls of the laity. It is not hard to see how an 'us and them'
attitude can develop, even with the best of intentions.

One of my favourite expressions regarding ministry, and indeed
regarding the Church in general, is the saying, 'We are all in this
together'. Everyone, clergy and laity, has something to teach, and
everyone has something to learn. This perspective does not sit comfortably with the traditional theology of priesthood, but it is essential
that priests and bishops recognise that they have as much to learn
from the laity, as the laity have to learn from them. Without this perspective, effective ministry is impossible.

Relating to 'Non-Club Members'

Just about everyone experiences some problems in relating. We all
feel a little anxious, meeting new people for the first time, perhaps
even meeting people we know well. It involves sharing something of
ourselves, exposing a little of who we are, and there's always a worry
about how the other person will respond, how they will accept what
we have shown them of ourselves.

For some it is more difficult than for others. Some people are by
nature more extroverted, in the sense that they enjoy being with people, whether in a group or on a one-to-one basis. Others are more
introverted, preferring their own company, or perhaps just a little shy,
and find dealing with people rather stressful.

For those who struggle with relating to others, and the stress that
it brings them, there is sometimes a tendency to act in certain ways to
try and overcome the problem, ways which unfortunately can cause
more problems for those around them. For example, sarcasm, play-

ing the clown, aloofness, moodiness, inappropriate humour, are just some of the ways that people deal with their difficulties in relating. They are not trying to make life difficult for others. It is just a coping mechanism that they have developed to deal with the stress. But what can happen, unfortunately, is that the coping mechanism very quickly becomes part of their personality and behaviour.

Priests and bishops are certainly not exempt from this phenomenon. In fact, it seems to me that among the clergy there is quite a high percentage of people who suffer from shyness, or who in some way experience difficulty in relating, especially to those other than fellow clergy.

I am not sure why this is the case. Perhaps the type of person who becomes a priest tends to be a bit of a 'loner'. They are certainly comfortable with remaining single, and they are also attracted by a contemplative, reflective lifestyle. Whatever the reason, the priest who tends to be introverted, rather than being people-orientated, needs to be very aware of that aspect of his personality, and be prepared to work on his relational skills, because the ability to relate well to parishioners, and others, is at the heart of his ministry.

Sometimes you see practical instances of priests or bishops having difficulty relating to those around them. One give away sign is when a new parish priest or administrator comes to a parish, and immediately feels the need to change things, to make his mark. This is not an uncommon occurrence. It happens also with bishops who come to a new diocese. Some bishops feel the need to change the way the diocese is organised, without looking at why those structures are set up in that way in the first place.

On the other hand, the priest or bishop who relates easily with people, comes to a new parish, or diocese, without feeling anxious, but wanting to work with the local people, getting to know them, and their ways of doing things, and allowing them to get to know himself, and what his thoughts and plans for the future might be. There is plenty of time for change, but it will be done collaboratively, with everyone working together, and sharing their talents.

Indeed, the mark of true leadership is not telling people what to do, but being able to bring people with you, all heading together with a common goal. And for that, one needs to be able to relate to a whole range of people, in a relaxed and confident way.

'Never Treat Them Like Sheep'

At one of my very first clergy gatherings, soon after my ordination, I was talking to an elderly priest from our diocese who was giving me some helpful advice about ministering in the parish. He was a wonderful man, gentle and wise. The part of our conversation that I remember best was when he said to me, 'John, in your priestly work, make sure you are a shepherd to your people, but never treat them like sheep'.

Unfortunately, I think we priests too often treat parishioners like sheep. It is not unusual to hear priests talking, in rather patronising terms, about their parishioners. It is not done in a spiteful way. It just comes out of an attitude that 'I am the priest, and I know what's best for them'.

I was once talking to a priest at one of our luncheons for the local clergy, and in our conversation he mentioned that he had just changed the Sunday Mass times in the parish. I asked what sort of a process he went through with the parishioners, to work out what were the best Mass times for everyone, but he responded that he did not consult with the parishioners at all. He believed he was the best person to make the decision, and so he made it. When I suggested that I would not change the Mass times without some sort of consultation process he responded with, 'But why not, you are the parish priest'. What was even more worrying was the fact that some of the other priests in the group, listening to the conversation, agreed with him.

Another way that the clergy can treat the laity like sheep is when bishops fail to inform the laity of new developments in Church teaching. The people in the pews are simply not brought into the conversation. Admittedly, Church teaching does not undergo a lot of change, but there are times when it is refined in some way. The notion of limbo is a typical example.

Anyone who grew up in a Catholic environment in the 1950s or 60s, or earlier, will be familiar with the idea of limbo. It was a place or state, where good people who were not baptised, and particularly infants, went after death. The argument was that since they were not baptised they could not go to heaven, but if they were good people, or, in the case of infants, they had never sinned at all, they could not go to hell. So, there must be another place, apart from purgatory, where these people go and enjoy eternity without any suffering, even though they cannot be with God in heaven.

It is true that limbo was never part of the formal doctrine of the Church, but it was certainly taught at the local level, and was in the Catholic catechism that was the basis of our Church teaching at the time.

Of course, the notion of limbo is not taught anymore at any level. Somewhere along the line it was quietly dropped. The word 'limbo' does not even appear in the catechism promulgated by Pope John Paul in 1992.

But no statement was ever put out, at least to my knowledge, to inform people that the notion of limbo was gone. Sadly, many people still worry about what happens to babies and young children who die before they are baptised, remembering what they were taught about limbo, and how unbaptised people could not go to heaven.

Of course, few people like admitting that they have changed their thinking on a particular topic. It does imply that their earlier opinion was inaccurate in some way, and needed to be corrected. I particularly understand why the bishops would not want to make it too obvious that the Church's teaching had undergone some rethinking. But surely this information needs to be said publicly, especially when it can allay the fears and concerns of many in the Catholic community.

Some years ago, I spoke at the Sunday Masses about the situation of Catholics who have been divorced, and whether they can receive Holy Communion. It had come to my attention that many Catholics were confused about the issue after a number of parishioners, in a short space of time, came to talk to me about the topic. Many people still thought that a divorced Catholic, who had not remarried, was somehow excluded from receiving Holy Communion. On a particular Sunday I spoke about the issue, and I also printed off some sheets and put them in the foyer of the church, explaining how there was no barrier whatsoever to people in that situation receiving Communion.

Shortly after, I was at a luncheon at the cathedral and I was talking to one of the bishops about the issue, and telling him how I had spoken at the Masses and how I had put out the sheets explaining how divorced people who had not remarried were very welcome to come to Communion. But I also said how he, as the bishop, should be doing the same thing at the diocesan level, because people needed to know the Church's official position on the issue. His response was, 'Well, you put out your sheets', as much as to say, 'Isn't that enough?'

Clergy and laity must work together in a relationship that is based on trust, openness and honesty, whether it's about practical things such as changing Mass times, or important pastoral issues such as welcoming divorced people to Communion. Only then can we as a Church move forward in an effective and harmonious way.

The Clergy Bubble

Not long ago I was attending a one-day conference for the Sydney clergy. There were probably close to 200 priests and bishops present in the group. We were all sorts of shapes and sizes. We were all different ages, ranging from late 20s to early 90s. We covered the whole political and theological spectrum, from left wing liberals to right wing conservatives. We came from many different parts of the world, including Australia, Africa, Asia, Europe and America. But there were two things we all had in common—we were male and we were celibate.

As I looked around the room and listened to the discussion I could not help but notice how male, and how celibate, the meeting was, and indeed, how male, and how celibate, the discussion was.

At one point, we were talking about clergy formation, and individual members of the group were asked to comment on how we as clergy can improve the way we grow and develop as people, and as leaders in the Church. I made the comment that we need to be open to allowing lay people to have input into our formation process. I said that as clergy we tend to say, 'The laity really don't understand our issues, because they are not priests themselves'. But in fact it is quite the opposite. The laity actually see things in the clergy that the clergy themselves don't see, because the laity look at things from a different perspective, from outside the clergy bubble.

There were, in fact, about half a dozen lay people present at that conference, helping with the administration, and I suggested that if we asked those people, who had been listening to our discussions, to make some comments on what they had seen and heard, I am sure we would have been challenged by some very thought-provoking observations. Needless to say, there was no further discussion about my suggestion, even in relation to future conferences.

One of the characteristics of the clergy club mentality is a tendency to always want to 'go it alone'. Priests are very hesitant to ask for help. There is a sense that ordination gives you everything you need to solve any problem. You do not need to rely on anyone else, particularly on those outside the club.

Consultation

Some years ago, a new archbishop to the diocese addressed a gathering of the priests at a clergy conference, and at the end of his talk he said that he would be happy to take questions. The first priest to raise his hand asked the archbishop if he would be establishing a pastoral council in the archdiocese. The answer was no. Some years later the same question was asked of his successor, and again the answer was no.

A pastoral council at the archdiocesan level is the equivalent of a parish council at the local parish level. Both are advisory bodies. The archdiocesan pastoral council advises the archbishop, while the parish pastoral council advises the parish priest. Neither the archbishop, nor the parish priest, is obliged to take the advice of his pastoral council. But both of them get a chance to listen to informed and committed parishioners sharing their views on the Church, and that input is so important for good governance.

One thing that continually puzzles me is why there has never been an archdiocesan pastoral council in the Sydney Archdiocese, or indeed, why so many parish priests refuse to have parish councils in their own parishes. From my own experience, I know how important the advice and support of the pastoral council is, in helping to keep a parish dynamic and vibrant. Without the infusion of new ideas and new perspectives the parish priest just keeps doing the same things over and over again, trying to solve the same problems in the same way.

I have heard some parish priests say they do not have pastoral councils because, as they put it, 'I am going to make the decisions anyway, so why waste time going through an advisory process'. One might admire their honesty, but it's hardly the sort of model of leadership we want to see in the Church.

At the archdiocesan level, the archbishops may well argue that they get advice from many people, including the auxiliary bishops, the council of priests, and the numerous people working in the various offices in the chancery. This may be the case, but the problem is that all these people are in some way indebted to the archbishop. The only way that the archbishop will receive honest advice is through a committee of lay people, who are free to speak honestly and openly about any issue. Ultimately, that is what consultation is really about.

The word 'consult' can be interpreted in a number of ways, but sometimes I feel the Church hierarchy have given their own particular meaning to the word. Some years ago, at a council of priests meeting, the archbishop announced that he had decided to implement a new project in the Sydney Archdiocese. Some of the priests at the meeting suggested that at least the members of the council of priests should have been consulted on the project before the archbishop made his decision. The archbishop responded that the council of priests had in fact been consulted. 'You were the first to know', he said.

While consultation with the priests can be problematic, consultation with the laity is almost non-existent. When I was in my last parish the bishops decided it was time to update the Archdiocesan Pastoral Plan, a very worthwhile project. They began by consulting with the clergy and with the various Church agencies and chancery offices. This process took over twelve months. Over this time I attended a number of council of priests meetings, and at each meeting I would ask the same question of the bishops, 'When are the people in the parishes going to be consulted?' Each time I received the same response, 'Don't worry, the people in the parishes will be given every chance to respond'.

Finally, the parishes were notified that the consultation stage was about to begin for them, but they were given only six weeks to complete the consultation, and have their responses back to the chancery.

Clearly, it was impossible to do a full consultation in that period of time. Most parish councils only meet once a month, at the most. To try and prepare a consultation process, to put that process in place in the parish, to collate the results, and then to get it all back to the chancery within six weeks was simply unrealistic. In our own case we did our best, but it was done under very difficult circumstances.

If the bishops are serious about consultation, they need to give the same amount of time and support to the people in the parishes, as they do to the people who work in Church offices and Church agencies. While it's true that those who are not employed by the Church are freer to express their views, and one would expect that in a consultation process their comments would be more forthright, this should not be a reason for the bishops to avoid this type of broader consultation. Indeed, this is exactly the sort of input the bishops need to hear, input that is honest and unfettered.

Inability to Empathise with Laity

One of the most unfortunate policies that the Church has ever introduced, at least in Australia, must surely be the policy that only allowed a marriage to take place inside the church building if it was between two Catholics. If the Catholic was marrying someone of another faith, the ceremony had to take place in the sacristy, or even outside the church building.

I remember once a parishioner speaking to me about this issue, and he told me that many years ago, his daughter married a man who was not Catholic, and because the wedding took place in a small country church, and there was not enough room in the sacristy to accommodate the wedding party, the actual marriage ceremony took place outside, in an area behind the church. He then told me that, from that day, he never went back to church, after 'They made his daughter get married next to the garbage bins'.

There are so many people who still talk about this issue, even though it was discontinued decades ago. The hurt it caused runs deep, and the memory of it is long lasting.

I know they were different times, and a different religious culture. I know, too, that culture, particularly Church culture, is a very powerful thing, but it is still hard to understand how this custom could have continued for as long as it did. I am sure the bishops who put the policy in place were acting in good faith. They were not trying to hurt anybody. But one of the expressions of the clergy club mentality is an inability to empathise with the laity. The bishops and priests of that time were not able to see the issue from a lay perspective, and therefore not able to feel the hurt that these couples, and their families, were experiencing.

Still today, the failure of priests to empathise with parishioners causes continual tensions in many parishes, and reinforces the lay/clergy disconnect. Even a seemingly small thing, such as the priest admonishing parishioners for coming late to Mass, can be an expression of the clergy's inability to empathise. Priests usually do not need much time to get ready for Mass. They have no one to organise but themselves, and often live next door to the church. A priest who ticks off parishioners for arriving late for Mass, especially if it is a family group, is probably unaware of the time and effort needed to get children organised for travel. He should be celebrating the fact that they have got themselves to church at all.

Inability to Accept Criticism

I once wrote an article that was critical of the leadership style of the archbishop of the day. The article was printed in *The Sydney Morning Herald*. The archbishop asked me to come and see him, and talk about what I had written, which I was happy to do.

I was obviously a little anxious as we sat down to have our discussion. I had given some thought to the sort of things he might ask me, but I was totally unprepared for his opening words, 'Are you having a vocation crisis?'

At the time, it seemed a rather odd thing to say. The idea of leaving the priesthood had never crossed my mind, and there was certainly nothing in the article that would indicate a vocation crisis. In the context of the clergy club mentality, however, it makes perfect sense.

It is very difficult for many of the clergy to believe that someone who loves the Church could actually be critical of the way the Church is run. In the same way, they cannot understand how someone who has great respect for the hierarchy could actually be critical of decisions they make, or of their style of leadership. One of the basic rules of the clergy club is to not break ranks, under any circumstances. Even if you disagree, you remain silent, or at best, you say it privately, within the club, so that there is no outward appearance of disunity. Those who do speak out are labelled 'malcontents' and 'troublemakers'. They do not have the good of the Church at heart. They must have some hidden agenda they are trying to push.

As always, it is not a phenomenon that is restricted to the Church. All institutions try to protect themselves from criticism, and many leaders of institutions see any sort of criticism as an attack on themselves personally, rather than an attempt to improve the institution and bring about reform.

Professional Appraisal for Clergy

Within the Sydney Archdiocese there has been an ongoing debate, over many years, about whether members of the clergy should undergo professional appraisal. This involves allowing others to look at the way priests and bishops go about their ministry, and to make comments and suggestions about their strengths, and about areas where they could make improvements.

Those in favour of clergy appraisals argue that there is no reason why bishops and priests cannot be appraised in their work, in the same way that other professionals are. Those against the appraisal system argue that priests are in a unique category, by the very nature of their work, and it would be impossible to appraise how they minister. The example of hearing confessions is often brought up.

Some years ago a group of priests, including myself, met to discuss the idea of putting together an appraisal process for the clergy, with the aim of presenting it to the archbishop, in the hope that it might be adopted as part of our professional formation. The group came together regularly, and with the assistance of a number of people with expertise in the area, produced a simple and flexible appraisal process that the members of the group underwent themselves, and found to be a very positive and worthwhile experience.

Unfortunately, when we presented it to the archbishop at a council of priests meeting he was less than enthusiastic. He said that if priests wanted to do it voluntarily, that was fine, but he was not in favour of it being formally introduced into the archdiocese.

Other priests at the meeting also spoke against the appraisal concept. Most of them had little or no experience of the professional appraisal process, and really did not understand what it was about. Some saw it in a negative way, as a judgement about them personally, rather than an opportunity to have their strengths affirmed, and to be helped to see areas where they could be even more effective in their ministering. There was also the feeling among some that what the priest does cannot be described as 'work', and so should not be subject to scrutiny, as in other professions.

There is only so much you can do in these situations. We felt we had given it our best shot, but it was clearly not going to happen, at least not at that point in time.

Another opportunity presented itself some years later with the arrival of a new archbishop to the archdiocese. Again we presented our proposal at a council of priests meeting, but again the concept was rejected. The archbishop did say, as his predecessor had done, that if a priest wanted to take part in an appraisal process, he could do it voluntarily, but it would not be introduced formally into the archdiocese.

Interestingly, in the light of comments made by the recent Royal Commission into Institutional Responses to Child Sexual Abuse, the archdiocese is now more open to the notion of 'appraisals' as part of its policy for Ongoing Formation of Priests. There is still some opposition to the concept on the part of the clergy, but hopefully it will soon be accepted by all, and even welcomed, as an essential element in the ongoing formation of priests, deacons and bishops.

'A Humbler Church'

One of the comments made by a number of bishops in the light of the child sexual abuse revelations and the subsequent Royal Commission, is that out of all this, the Catholic Church will be a 'humbler church'. It is a statement that implies that the Church's leaders too, will be humbler leaders.

We all find it difficult to exercise the virtue of humility, but one can understand why bishops, in particular, might find it difficult to be humble, to admit their mistakes, to say sorry. They are the leaders of a Church, founded by Jesus, whose parting words were, 'And remember, I am with you always, to the end of the age' (Mt 28:20). How can the bishops make mistakes? How can they admit that they were wrong? Surely the Holy Spirit is guiding them. Will it look like they have lost their way? Will the parishioners lose faith in the Church? Will they lose faith in God?

Because of this pressure, many bishops feel a necessity to be always in control, and to have all the answers. It is not done out of arrogance, but from a perceived need to present the Church as being divine, and infallible. Unfortunately, it is not an attitude that sits well with the virtue of humility. It is also not an attitude that makes it easy to admit one's mistakes, or to say 'I am truly sorry'.

The story of the astronomer Galileo, and his relationship with the Church, is one of many examples where the Church hierarchy has struggled to be open to people who are genuinely striving to find the truth, even if they may be coming at it from a different perspective. It happened a long time ago admittedly, but the attitude of the hierarchy is substantially the same.

Galileo, through his research and astronomical observations, was reaching the conclusion that the earth was not the central planet, around which the other heavenly bodies revolved. His theory clashed with Church teaching, which supported the view that since humanity is the high point of God's creation, as shown in the Scriptures, the earth must therefore have been created at the centre of the universe. The crucial point in the whole Galileo debate was that the bishops only needed to look into the telescope, and they would have seen for themselves that Galileo was on the right track. Instead, they maintained that they had no need to look into the telescope, they knew they were right.

In 1992 Pope John Paul II formally apologised to Galileo, on behalf of the Church. It was good that the apology was made, but it was hundreds of years too late.

More recently, and closer to home, the hierarchy's difficulty in apologising for mistakes made by the Church can be seen in the way the bishops respond to the victims of sexual abuse by clergy.

I must say at the outset, that from my perspective, the bishops genuinely believe they are doing everything they can to redress the terrible damage done to the victims of clergy sexual abuse. Certainly, the bishops I have spoken to, feel a great sense of sorrow and remorse for what has happened and are determined to do all they can to make sure nothing of the kind ever happens again.

But there seems to be a problem in how they express that sorrow and remorse. It doesn't seem to come across as truly heartfelt, and sometimes ends up being a sort of 'Church-speak', instead of words that people can truly relate to. Perhaps it's the case that the clergy are not good at expressing their feelings. Living a celibate lifestyle means you don't get a lot of practice at it.

Whatever the reasons, there certainly does seem to be a serious disconnect between the Church hierarchy and the victims of clergy sexual abuse. One can only hope that through the work of the Royal Commission, and the efforts of the Church itself, and especially its leaders, that disconnect will disappear.

Grumpy Priests

I sometimes wonder why priests cannot be more joyful, and actually look like they enjoy what they are doing. Certainly, there are some who do, and their parishioners are very grateful. But it is not the norm. Many priests almost seem to go out of their way to make life difficult for their parishioners, or at the very least, they could be described as grumpy.

Some years ago a family came to our parish to ask if their child could join our First Communion program. They had been unable to attend the first lesson in their own parish, and the parish priest would not let the child participate in the remainder of the program. We did a forty minute catch up lesson with the family, and the child continued in our program, and made her First Communion with us.

It is not hard to work with families who, overwhelmingly, come to the Church with goodwill. It just takes a little flexibility, and a belief that, by and large, everyone is doing their best in the circumstances they find themselves in. You don't have to be grumpy and rigid. It does nothing for either the priest himself, or for the people he is upsetting.

I was once at a clergy meeting and the priests were asked if there was anything they would like to bring up for discussion. One priest complained that there were people coming to Anointing Masses who, he thought, were not really sick. These people, he said, should not be receiving the sacrament. I remember thinking to myself, of all the issues you could take up, yours has to be stopping people from receiving the sacrament of the Anointing because you think they are not sick enough.

One of the constant complaints from couples getting married is that the priest won't allow them to use 'secular' music. It is almost as if anything other than traditional Church music is somehow sinful. Of course, the music needs to be appropriate, and we are not talking about music that is crude or tasteless. But not to allow a couple to choose music for their ceremony that clearly means something to them, seems to me to be a little mean-spirited, and even somewhat obsessive.

Life is always about flexibility and compromise. You cannot always get your own way, and you shouldn't always try to, or expect it. Relationships develop and grow because people are willing to give and take. If the clergy want their relationship with the laity to grow and develop, they will have to approach it in that spirit, with a positive attitude, and a smile on their faces.

Two Standards

For a number of years there was a priest in a Sydney parish who would not baptise a child if the parents were not married. There is nothing in canon law, or any other Church law, to say that parents must be married before they can have their child baptised. This particular priest just made up his own rule, and refused to budge.

I brought up the matter at a council of priests meeting and, without naming the priest in question, I suggested to the archbishop that he put a note in the clergy newsletter to remind the priests that, while there may indeed be grounds for not baptising a child, the marital state of the parents is not one of them.

Unfortunately, the note never appeared in the newsletter. The clergy club is a very tight-knit group, and when it comes to a choice between supporting your fellow clergy, or supporting the laity, the clergy seem to win out every time, even when it is obvious to everyone that it is the priest who is in the wrong.

Recently during one of the sessions of the Royal Commission into Institutional Responses to Child Sexual Abuse, an Australian bishop compared the legal responsibility of the Church hierarchy towards victims of clergy sexual abuse, to that of the owner of a trucking company who learns that one of his drivers has picked up a woman and molested her.[1] Perhaps the bishop is technically correct. The legal responsibility of the Church hierarchy for the crimes of the clergy seems to be quite minimal, but the moral responsibility is not. Bishops have a pastoral concern for parishioners, and especially for children, that the owner of a trucking company does not have.

The bishop was clearly trying to downplay the responsibility of the Church hierarchy in the sexual abuse crisis. It should not be surprising that the clergy would close ranks and support one another when they feel under threat. But they rarely show that same support for the laity. In fact, the 'sins' of the laity are treated far more harshly than those of the clergy, even extending to them being excluded from Holy Communion. It is a double standard, and it expresses itself often in the club mentality.

Lack of Complaints Procedure

In society generally, whether in private enterprise or in government institutions, when someone has a complaint to make, there is often a

---

1. Cardinal George Pell appearing at the Royal Commission into Institutional Responses to Child Sexual Abuse, via video link from the Vatican, reported in the Sydney Morning Herald, 22 August 2014.

process or a forum whereby they can air their grievance, and have it followed through in an appropriate way. The processes are not always perfect, but there are certainly guidelines in place.

Sadly, there are no such procedures in place in the Church. I am not talking here about criminal matters. I am referring to a situation where, for example, a school principal may not be happy with the expectations that the parish priest puts on the school staff, or a priest may not be happy with the way he has been treated by his bishop. There are no formal processes through which these sorts of issues can be addressed.

In the case of principals of parish schools, if they feel they, or members of the school community, have been treated unfairly by the parish priest, they are certainly able to go to the appropriate person within the school system and air their complaint, but that is where the process ends. The priest is always supported, and the school principal or teacher is told that they just have to put up with it. I have seen situations myself where this has happened, and I have had many teachers tell me the same thing.

In the case of priests who feel they have been treated unfairly by the bishop, the situation is much the same. The only thing the priest can really do is to have a meeting with the bishop, and hope he can get him to see his point of view. Ultimately the power is with the bishop, and decisions are made sometimes without recourse to objective evidence.

Once at a council of priests meeting, I noticed that a discussion from the previous meeting had been inaccurately recorded in the minutes. In that previous discussion the archbishop had been arguing for a particular proposal, but there had also been some strong arguments put against the proposal. In the minutes, however, only the archbishop's arguments had been recorded. I raised my hand and objected to the way the minutes had been recorded, and maintained that both sides of the argument should have been recorded. The archbishop agreed that the discussion had not been recorded accurately, but the minutes were never amended.

Ultimately the bishop is a law unto himself, and without any procedures in place to address complaints or grievances that situation will never change.

It is also interesting that the secretary who was taking the minutes at that meeting was a lay person, employed by the archdiocese, and clearly it was in his best interests to support the position of the archbishop.

If it is difficult for members of the clergy or school principals to have their voices heard in the Church, it is even more difficult for a parishioner to have a grievance listened to. Over the years I have had numerous parishioners tell me of letters they have written to the bishop regarding issues they have felt strongly about, but have received very little in the way of a response. In many cases the letters weren't even answered.

Putting a complaints procedure in place in the archdiocese would not be unduly difficult. It has been done in response to sexual abuse complaints, but there are other complaints that also require attention, where people have been treated unfairly by members of the clergy, and deserve to have their grievances heard.

A Corporate Church

One of the comments that is being made more and more about our local Church is that it is becoming corporate, in the sense that it is starting to resemble a legal or financial institution, more than a Church. Admittedly there is a lot more administrative work to do than there was in the past, but no amount of administration can determine an attitude. Only people determine attitudes.

There is a place in the Church, an important place, for the finance people, and the legal people, and the administrative people in general, but that aspect of the Church must never override the pastoral work of the Church, which is at the centre of its mission. In today's world particularly, it is important that the Church never yields to the temptation to corporatise. If it looks like a business, it probably is, and we have clearly lost our way.

Pomp and Ceremony

During my studies in Rome in the 1990s I went to a papal audience. It was the first time I had ever been to one, and I was a little unsure of what to expect. I had gone with some Italian friends of mine and as we sat, waiting in a large hall for Pope John Paul II to arrive, I noticed a musical band at the side of the stage starting to warm up, and next to them a bishop in his cassock trying to get the crowd revved up for the pope's entry. We were all being encouraged to clap, and make plenty of noise.

I had never seen anything like it before at a Church gathering, and I had trouble making sense of it. Why were we being encouraged to give the pope a 'pop star' welcome? Of course, the pope has a very special place in the Church and should be greeted with respect and enthusiasm, but this performance smacked of triumphalism, and to me, said all the wrong things about who we are as a Church, and who the pope is as our servant-leader.

Triumphalism is a constant temptation for the Church, as much today as it has been in the past. Indeed, it is a temptation for all of us to blow our own trumpet, and the dynamic seems to be even stronger in communities and institutions. We all want to present ourselves as successful and important, triumphant, we could say, and the Church is no exception.

The most obvious expression of this attitude within the Church is in the liturgy. The liturgy is the formal, public worship and prayer of the Church. Most people's experience of the liturgy is through the Mass and the sacraments. The liturgy should be reverent, respectful and prayerful, and it should express always our relationship with God, and God's relationship with us.

Sometimes when I attend liturgies, particularly in cathedrals, the pomp and ceremony is so extreme that I wonder whether the celebration has become more about the liturgical ministers, than it is about the worship, or at least more about the liturgical actions themselves, rather than about their meaning. Even the furniture appears a bit self-serving. The priest or bishop sits on what is called the 'presidential chair' during Mass, but I have seen many such chairs in churches and cathedrals that look more like thrones than chairs.

Then there are the vestments that priests buy, sometimes at huge expense. I think I would be on safe ground suggesting that there would be enough vestments in church sacristies, at least in Australia, to adequately supply all our priests, three times over. I am not sure why we need more.

Of course, the reason given for why these things are necessary for the liturgy is that they are for God, and God deserves them. I know we all see God differently, but certainly the God I know is not interested in throne-like chairs and gold-braided chasubles.

The Sign of Peace

In 2004 the Congregation for Divine Worship and the Discipline of the Sacraments issued an Instruction entitled *Redemptionis Sacramentum*.[2] It was subtitled 'On certain matters to be observed or to be avoided regarding the Most Holy Eucharist'. One of the issues it addressed was the way the priest was to offer the sign of peace at Mass.

Up to that time it was customary for the priest, after he had given the sign of peace to the ministers on the sanctuary, to go and give the sign of peace to a few members of the congregation in the front pew. In the instruction, however, this has been forbidden. In paragraph 72 it states that 'The Priest may give the sign of peace to the ministers but always remains within the sanctuary, so as not to disturb the celebration'.

I understand where the decision is coming from. The Congregation for Divine Worship is concerned that the sign of peace may become too informal and too extended, and so take away from the solemnity of the Communion rite. But surely the priest coming to the people in the pews and giving a sign of peace is a powerful symbol of the unity of the worshipping community. And it is especially significant when so much else in the Mass, at least from a liturgical perspective, suggests a separation between, on the one hand, the priest and ministers on the sanctuary, and on the other hand, the rest of the congregation in the body of the church. The altar rails used to be the physical barrier between the priest and the congregation. Maybe it is the case now that while the altar rails are no longer present in most churches, the altar rail mentality is still there.

It is also interesting to note that, to the best of my knowledge, no formal notice was given in the diocese regarding this change in practice. The first inkling I had was when I noticed that some of the bishops who came to the parish for Confirmation were no longer giving the sign of peace to anyone in the congregation. I asked a few of my priest friends if they knew anything about it, and one mentioned that he thought something might have come out from Rome on the subject. I followed it up and found the relevant document. I can't help thinking that even the bishops were a little embarrassed about publi-

---

cising it. It is not a good look when the hierarchy makes a ruling that forbids the priest from giving the sign of peace to a few people in the front pew at Mass.

The reason for the ruling is also interesting, 'so as not to disturb the celebration'. From my perspective, it is hard to see how the priest and a few members of the congregation offering each other the sign of peace could 'disturb the celebration'. Rather, I would see the gesture as forming part of the celebration. I can't imagine that at the Last Supper Jesus did not give some type of sign of peace to his disciples, and I'm sure it did not disturb the celebration.

The sign of peace issue is certainly not the most pressing issue facing the Church, but it is just another expression, among many, of the disconnection between the clergy and the laity.

New Translation

For many centuries, up until the time of the Second Vatican Council, the Mass had been celebrated in Latin all around the world. Then, at the Second Vatican Council, the momentous decision was made to have the Mass celebrated in the vernacular, that is, in the language of the country or region in which the Mass is being celebrated. Once the decision was made, the various language groups then quickly got to work to translate the Mass texts into their own national languages.

The English translation first appeared in the Mass in 1969 and that text was used, with minor changes, until 2011. The translation is not perfect by any means, either in the accuracy of the translation from the Latin, or in its literary style, although, it must be said, that given the enormity of the task, and the speed with which it was produced, it was a job well done, and the translation has served the English-speaking Church well for over forty years.

That said, it was clear that an updating of the translation was necessary, and we all looked forward to what would be produced. This time the translators were not under the same time restraints as their predecessors, and so we anticipated a sound translation that was faithful to the Latin texts, while at the same time written in a style that was contemporary and easy to understand.

For many of us, however, anticipation quickly turned to dismay, and even disbelief, when the first media reports started to come through, citing references from the new text. It was soon becoming obvious that the new translation would be little more than a 'latinised' version of English, translated literally from the original Latin, with little attention given to English literary style or syntax.

When the final text was published, the overwhelming sentiment was that it was not only unpleasant to the ear, but also often quite difficult to understand, due mainly to the awkwardness of its phrasing and the use of archaic language.

I remember once, soon after the new translation had been introduced, a priest who had celebrated four weekend Masses saying to me, 'I said that preface four times this weekend, and I still don't know what it's saying'. More recently, another priest told me that after checking over the prayers for the upcoming Sunday Mass, he felt they were so laboured and cumbersome that he went and found a copy of the old missal and used it for the Sunday Masses.

I had my own experience recently when I was celebrating Sunday Mass in the parish, and I read this particular prayer from the new missal—'Receive our oblation, O Lord, by which is brought about a glorious exchange, that, by offering what you have given, we may merit to receive your very self.' It is actually a very beautiful prayer, but the contrived and antiquated language distracts from the prayer itself. The same prayer, in the old translation, reads as follows—'Lord, accept our sacrifice as a holy exchange of gifts. By offering what you have given us may we receive the gift of yourself.'

I know the bishops will argue that the New Translation version is more appropriate for the Mass because it follows more closely the Latin of the original prayer, but to me, the version we have used for decades is eminently more preferable. It says the same thing, but in a way that is not only easier to understand, but more pleasant to the ear.

But perhaps even more worrying than the language in the new translation is the mentality behind the language, a mentality that harks back to the days of the old Latin Mass. Clearly, those responsible for the final text wanted it to reflect the tone of a past era. In fact, one of the bishops on the translation commission told a group of Sydney priests that his own personal preference was to say Mass facing the tabernacle, as it was done in the pre-Vatican II Church.

There are many different models of Church, and certainly the pre-Vatican II model is having a resurgence among some of the clergy today. It is not up to me to criticise their position, even though I may take a different one. But what does concern me is that the pre-Vatican

II model of Church is very alienating for many Catholics. The vast majority of the laity do not wish to go back to a pre-Vatican Church. The vast majority of the laity do not like the new translation. The vast majority of the laity do not want priests and bishops celebrating Mass with their backs to the people, if for no other reason, than just to keep their children coming to Mass.

I know there are some among the clergy who disagree with this view, and believe that if they can make the contemporary Church look more like the pre-Vatican Church, people will start coming back to Mass, and the Church will return to the glory days of the 1950s. I have to say I see no evidence of this, after more than thirty years of parish experience in a variety of parishes. Yes, there is a small percentage of the laity, including young people, who prefer the older, more conservative model of Church, but they are in the minority. The vast majority of the laity want a Church that is modern and progressive. They want to be able to pray in contemporary English, not in language from the past, and they want their priests to be normal, happy, and not overly clerical.

Club Language

Language is such an important part of our culture, and such an influential tool for getting our message across. The institutional language used by the hierarchy says a lot about how bishops see the world, how they see God, and how they see the laity. I will begin with the issue of inclusive language.

Inclusive language refers to the use of words and phrases that explicitly include both men and women, rather than using a single male term, such as 'men', to refer to both genders. It is a particular issue in writings used by the Church because so much of the Church's language, particularly its liturgical language, has its origins in texts that were written many centuries ago, when women were treated as second class citizens. Sadly, that former attitude towards women is still reflected in the language of the Church today.

It is often noted that, regarding inclusive language, the Church is still struggling with an issue that society has dealt with, and from which it has moved on. While there may be still some way to go, by and large inclusive language has become the norm in everyday life. Certainly, a public speaker who used terms like 'men' or 'brothers' to refer to both men and women, would not only be criticised for doing so, but would be seen as reflecting an attitude from a bygone era.

In the Church, however, things are different. In our liturgical prayers and readings we are still using male terms to describe men and women. In the Nicene Creed, for example, the congregation at Sunday Mass still says 'for us men and for our salvation he came down from heaven', while the reader at Mass still uses the term 'brothers', for example, in St Paul's letters, when referring to the whole Christian community of men, women and children. I know that in some versions of the Bible the word 'brothers' is now translated as 'brothers and sisters', or even 'neighbours', but in the Jerusalem Bible version used at Catholic Masses in Australia, the word 'brothers' is still the translation.

Of course, the argument put forward is that the original words form part of the Church's Scripture and its tradition, and therefore cannot be changed. But this always seems to me to be an argument without great merit. The Church leaders who formulated the Nicene Creed clearly intended to say that Jesus brought salvation to both men and women, even though in the culture of the day, the term 'men' was sufficient to get that message across. In the same way, the term 'brothers' in St Paul refers to all those in the community, men, women and children. So, the irony is that inclusive terms such as 'men and women' and 'brothers and sisters' are actually closer to the meaning of the original texts, than are the male terms that are currently used.

Another aspect of our liturgical language that concerns me is how we continue to publicly read things from Scripture that are no longer appropriate, and even sometimes offensive. St Paul's statement from his letter to the Ephesians that women should obey their husbands and be subject to them, is a typical example (Eph 5:22). Every time the passage is read at Mass there are some smiles, perhaps a few nudges between husbands and wives, and also a few cringes, as people try to deal with a statement that is clearly outdated, and arguably inappropriate in such a setting. We have moved a long way since the time those words were written, a time when vulnerable people were used as slaves, and women were seen as men's possessions. Today slavery in any form is banned in any civilised country, and women are seen as having the same dignity and rights as men. But if we, as a Church, keep repeating inappropriate statements from a bygone era, we are, at best, appearing somewhat ambiguous about issues of basic justice.

In the Gospel reading about Jesus feeding the people with the bread and the fish, there is a line that finishes with 'and those who ate were about five thousand men, besides women and children' (Mt14:21). In the Jerusalem Bible version the last phrase is translated as 'not counting women and children'. I have for years refused to say that last phrase when I read that particular Gospel passage at Mass. I find it offensive, and I know there are others in the Church who feel the same. At the time the Gospel was written, women and children were not counted in a crowd because of their low standing in society. But if we continue to repeat those words today, we are, at least implicitly, projecting the same message.

The problems surrounding inclusive language are certainly not insurmountable by any standards. There just seems to be a lack of will, and even worse, a lack of interest.

Language about God

Once, at a talk I was giving on inclusive language, I read some prayers from the Mass liturgy, and wherever the term 'Father' appeared, relating to God, I substituted the word 'Mother'. It is a very interesting thing to do, and reminds us how much our liturgical language is male language, not just in the words used, but in the concepts and images behind the words. Phrases such as 'O God, Almighty Mother', and 'All-powerful Mother', seem odd, not just because we are unfamiliar with using female terms for God, but because the terms themselves have an inner incongruity. The words 'power' and 'might' have definite male overtones, and don't fit easily with the notion of mother.

Of course, some will argue that you cannot use female terms to refer to God, because God is not female. I have even had a bishop tell me not to refer to God with female terms. Such comments do seem to imply a belief in a God who actually does have a gender. Clearly that cannot be the case. A God with gender cannot be an infinite God.

We struggle to find a language to describe God, and a language to use when we pray to God, because we can only think in male and female terms. God is clearly neither male nor female. The reason for using male terms for God is certainly historical, but it is also cultural.

Today our culture, particularly western culture, is becoming less patriarchal, and more inclusive of women, and so there is no reason why we cannot use both male and female terms to describe God. It would certainly allow us to think about God in a fuller way, and help us to reflect on qualities of God that are rarely considered, and even more rarely mentioned.

Trying to get our bishops to even engage in the discussion, however, has proved to be a very difficult project. They are clearly very comfortable with male language for God, and see no reason to change. I cannot help but think that the "maleness" of the clergy club has some bearing on the bishops' attitude, and on their insistence that only male terms be used in reference to God.

Resistance to Change

It is sometimes said that in modern society, change is the only constant. It is certainly a fundamental part of our world, and it brings its own challenges, for everyone. Church leaders, in particular, do not find the notion of change an easy one to deal with. The Church's theology, and philosophy, is heavily influenced by the scholars from the Middle Ages, and their thinking was characterised in many ways by certainty and constancy.

Natural law is still the basis for much of the reasoning found in papal documents, and in the writings of local bishops. According to natural law, moral principles are inherent in nature, and thus unchanging. They can also be universally understood through human reason. Clearly, such a view of the world does not sit easily with contemporary philosophy, where the world is seen as far more complex and uncertain.

The same-sex marriage issue is a good example of the bishops' use of natural law theology. The Church's position, that marriage should only be between a man and a woman, is straight-forward and unchanging. It is based on the different physical natures of men and women, and the fact that, through their union, children are produced.

The counter argument is more empirical. People of the same gender can love each other just as much as those of different genders, and so should also be allowed to express that love and commitment through marriage. They may not be able to have children from their own relationship, but there are many blended families around today.

It's easy to see how the two sides have so much trouble finding any common ground. It's also easy to see how Church leaders struggle to find any merit in the more empirical approach. That has never been the hierarchy's way of thinking.

I was listening to a bishop speaking to a group of priests on the topic of same-sex marriage. He was very black and white, and very sure of the validity of his arguments. As I listened to him I was tempted to put my hand up and ask, 'Do you ever feel that you might be wrong?'

I do not know the answers to all these moral dilemmas, but I cannot help thinking that we all, including our Church leaders, need to be a little more open to listening to a whole range of views on contemporary issues, even if some of those positions may be at variance with more traditional Church views.

Life is not always as simple and straight-forward as we would like it to be. It will always be full of ambiguity and paradox, uncertainty and doubt. To deny those realities is to not only live in an artificial world, but to distance ourselves from the lives of so many around us.

Of course, we must hold firm to the views we believe are true, but we must also be open to the fact that we may not always be right, every time, whether we are laity or clergy, priest or cardinal, or even the pope. As I have already noted, a sense of certainty and constancy is indicative of the clergy club mentality, but surely this cannot help in dealing with the complex and challenging issues that are continually presenting themselves in our contemporary society.

Interpretation of Scripture

I can still remember the day when I first heard that there may not really have been an Adam and Eve, and humanity may not have started with the two of them in the Garden of Eden, along with a snake and a fruit tree. I was still in primary school, probably in about year 5 or 6. We often used to read Bible stories at school, and like most children at the time, we believed that the events happened just as they were recorded in the Bible.

But now they were telling us something different. The events may not have happened like that at all. Perhaps they were stories told to get a message across, rather than strict historical narratives. It was certainly a shock to a young child, but of course, as I grew older and learnt more about the Scriptures I came to understand that we cannot take all of the Bible literally.

This question about how literally we can interpret the Bible is a continual area of controversy within the Church. Did God really kill the first-born children of the Egyptians? I suggest that most Scripture scholars would say no. Did the bodies of dead people come back to life and get out of their graves when Jesus died on Calvary? Once again, the majority of scholars would not take this passage literally. Were these events, and many like them in the Bible, stories told to get across a message about faith? Almost certainly.

The way we interpret Scripture says a lot about our openness to new ways of looking at the stories of our faith. Whether we are in primary school, or are much older, it can be somewhat unnerving when we first realise that the Bible is primarily a book about faith, not history, and that the messages about faith are far more important than the historical accuracy of the stories.

At the institutional level this discovery can be even more unnerving. It is easy to see why the bishops would not welcome a perspective that suggests many of the stories in the Bible are not accurate accounts of what actually happened, and the events in some of the stories may not have happened at all. What will people think? Will they think that none of the Bible is true?

It is not surprising then that the Church hierarchy is slow to support modern scripture scholarship. Rarely do you hear bishops question the historical accuracy of the Scriptures. Priests in their homilies still talk about sick people being cured by having devils driven out of them, because that is what it actually says in the gospel account. The story of the boy with epilepsy in Matthew's gospel (Mt 17:14) is a typical example. But surely priests should also mention in their homilies, at least occasionally, that today, with modern medical knowledge, we know what epilepsy is, and it has nothing to do with devils.

In all of this, the clergy club mentality is at work, holding on to past certainties, and hesitant to open up new ways of looking at the stories of our faith. And so, everyone is a loser, clergy and laity alike, because without being challenged by new ways of looking at God and Jesus, which modern Scripture scholarship provides, we fail to grow in our faith, restrained in a world view from the first century.

Reaching Out to the Educated

The correlation between poverty, lack of formal education, and religious fervour does not happen by chance. Religion tends to flourish in communities that do not subject their faith to rigid intellectual scrutiny. By contrast, people who are more formally educated, often challenge religious principles that seem to go against accepted rational thinking. It is not surprising then, that the fall-off in religious practice is greater in countries with higher, rather than lower, educational levels.

This trend is most concerning and deserves serious reflection. I know some argue that countries with a high standard of education are wealthier, and with wealth comes consumerism and materialism, and so people are less focussed on the bigger realities of faith and eternity. There may be some truth in this argument, but I don't think it is the full story.

Rather, I believe that the way our faith is presented by the Church hierarchy makes it difficult for rational, educated people to accept. Having to believe in biblical stories about miracles and supernatural phenomenon should not be a prerequisite for becoming part of the Christian community. In the same way, having to believe in doctrinal statements that, at best, test the limits of rational thinking, should not be necessary to be able to practice Christian faith.

Let me take one example. In 1950 Pope Pius XII declared the doctrine of the Assumption an infallible statement, that is, to be believed by all Catholics. The doctrine states that Mary, the mother of Jesus, at the end of her life was taken up to heaven 'body and soul'. What does this mean exactly? How can someone's body, Mary's or anyone else's, be taken up to heaven? Human bodies are physical entities. Heaven is not.

I have often asked this question of clergy, along with other questions about various doctrinal statements that seem to conflict with human experience, and the answer I regularly get is, 'Oh, but that is doctrine', as if we have to somehow suspend our reason when it comes to Church matters.

Bishops and priests may be prepared to do this, but many of the laity are not. And for this reason, I feel it is important that both Scripture and doctrine are presented in ways that are more in keeping with modern scholarship and modern thinking, and less in keeping with the scholarship and thinking of a medieval world. Otherwise we will, as a Church, continue to find it difficult to connect with the increasing number of educated people who are searching for meaning in life.

Legalism

Not long before I was ordained, our class gathered at a small chapel in the seminary to celebrate Mass. There were nine of us in the group, plus the priest on the seminary staff who was leading the celebration. Just as we were about to begin, the priest noticed that the altar breads we were using for Mass were all of the smaller variety, and we did not have one of the larger altar breads that the priest traditionally uses for Mass. I could not see why it would make any difference but it was decided that we could not begin Mass without having one of the large altar breads, so one of the group had to go off to get one. He obviously had difficulty tracking one down, because he was away for a long time, but finally he returned, and we were able to begin Mass.

I always think of that incident as a good example of what legalism is. In terms of celebrating Mass, it makes no difference how big the altar breads are. The reason the priest uses a larger altar bread when celebrating Mass in the parish is so that it can be seen by the congregation, some of whom may be sitting a long way from the altar. For the ten of us sitting in a circle in that small chapel, there was no issue about seeing the altar bread. It was just that the priest had been so used to using a large host that he was no longer able to say Mass without one.

I once celebrated a wedding where the bride had been married twice before. The previous two marriages had ended in divorce, and because on those two occasions she had married in churches other than the Catholic Church, without getting permission to do so, the marriages were quickly annulled, requiring only a couple of weeks to get the paperwork processed. Her third marriage therefore, was able to take place in the Catholic Church.

After the wedding ceremony I was speaking to one of the bridesmaids, who told me that this was the third time she had been a bridesmaid at her friend's wedding. Then she added, with tears in her eyes, that she herself was divorced, but since she had done the right thing in the first place, and had her wedding ceremony in the Catholic Church, she was unable to get an annulment and marry again in the Catholic Church as her friend had.

The problem with legalism is that it allows the law to become an end in itself. Laws are never meant to be like that. Laws exist to ensure that people are treated fairly and justly, and that no one receives special treatment over another. This needs to be constantly taken into account with regard to the Church's canon law, particularly when framing laws about marriage.

I mention this because many of the clergy seem to be caught up with the Church's law in a way that the laity are not. Perhaps it is because of all those years studying canon law in the seminary. Perhaps it is because the law is black and white, and thus gives a sense of safety and security. Perhaps it is because the priest is the expert in Church law. Whatever the reason, it is important that our Church hierarchy formulates, and puts into practice, the laws of the Church in such a way that they remain always at the service of the people, and not at the service of the institution.

I was at a meeting of priests once, just after Pope Francis had announced some changes to the marriage annulment process which would make the procedure a little simpler and quicker. At the meeting the priests were discussing the changes, and a number of them were not in favour of what the pope had done. They felt it was making the process of getting an annulment too easy. The discussion went on for quite some time, without any reference to the couples who were trying to sort out their broken relationships, and get on with their lives. I could not help thinking that this was the clergy club mentality in action, in a group of priests, with the best intentions in the world, unable to look beyond the institution, and see the people for whom the institution was founded.

Binding and Loosening

I used to regularly visit one of the auxiliary bishops in the archdiocese, and over time we became quite friendly. He was a very perceptive man. He said many wise things to me but one thing in particular will always stay in my mind. It was in reference to the passage in Matthew's Gospel when Jesus said to Peter, 'Whatever you bind on earth will be bound in heaven, and whatever you loose on earth will be loosed in heaven' (Mt 18:18). What the bishop said to me was, 'The Church is very good at binding, but not so good at loosening'.

Up to that time I had never really thought about the 'loosening' part of that passage. But when you look at it, Jesus directive to loosen is every bit as solemn and as strong as his directive to bind.

I tend to think that our bishops see themselves more as 'binders' than 'looseners'. I sometimes get the sense that they see binding as a strength, and loosening as a weakness. In fact, over the last thirty years I am struggling to think of many things that would affect people's lives in any significant way, that have been loosened in the Church. I can think of plenty that have been kept bound.

The clergy club mentality expresses itself in many ways. Binding is one of them.

The Seal of Confession

Many years ago, in one of my seminary classes, we were looking at the question of absolutes. What is absolute? Are there any absolutes apart from God? One of the students in the class suggested that the seal of Confession was an absolute, not able to be broken under any circumstances whatsoever?

As I reflected on this issue I thought of possible scenarios that might render even the seal of Confession non-absolute. What if a priest was told in confession by a penitent that he had set a bomb that was due to explode that day, killing hundreds of people. Would the priest be able to act on that information to save the lives of those hundreds of innocent people?

The question about whether or not the seal of confession can be broken has taken on new meaning with the Royal Commission into Institutional Responses to Child Abuse. It could well be the case that a paedophile priest comes to the sacrament of Reconciliation to confess that he has been sexually abusing children over a long period of time. Perhaps he has come to confession as a cry for help. Perhaps he genuinely believes that he has changed his ways and will not offend again. Whatever the motivation, the priest hearing the confession is put in an extraordinarily difficult position. The offending priest comes back to confession on a regular basis, confessing the same sin of sexual abuse of children. He is continually urged to go to the police and confess his crime, but it never happens. What does the priest confessor do? Can he inform the police, or must he remain silent?

Every time I have put this question to members of the clergy, the answer has always been the same. The priest must remain silent. The seal of Confession cannot be broken under any circumstances. It is the long-held view of the Church hierarchy, and backed up by canon law. There are no exceptions, and no discussion is ever entered in to.

But is this really the way it should be? Is it wrong to question whether a bishop or priest must remain silent, knowing that young children are being systematically sexually abused? Is the seal of Confession more important than the welfare of those children?

Catholic moral theology has for centuries used a principle known as 'double effect' to try and deal with these types of dilemmas. The principle of double effect asserts that an action is permissible, even if it is seriously harmful, providing the harm is a side effect of the intended good. The good must outweigh the harm, and the harm cannot be directly intended. Numerous examples can be cited, such as the administration of medication to relieve the pain of a terminally ill patient, even though it is clear that the medication will hasten the patient's death. Another example is killing in self-defence, where the direct intention is to save one's life. The crucial, and subjective, element in the argument is whether the intended good outweighs the harm that is caused.

The Church hierarchy continue to argue that the good that is done by protecting the children from sexual abuse does not outweigh the harm that is done by breaking the seal of Confession. To me this seems to be a very clerical argument. Indeed, I would suggest that this particular issue, perhaps more than most, highlights the disconnection that exists between clergy and laity, and the fact that so many priests and bishops look at the world very differently to the way most other people do. No one is denying that confidentiality in Confession is extremely important. No one is denying that the sacrament of Reconciliation is a most significant part of the life of the Church. But neither of them is an end in itself. Surely it is not beyond reason to suggest that the protection of children from sexual abuse is at least as important, if not more important, than the protection of the seal of Confession.

It is certainly a very sensitive and contentious issue, but one that must be discussed openly by the Church hierarchy, with both sides of the argument taken into consideration. It can no longer be put in the 'too hard' basket, or simply be treated as 'non-negotiable'.

Inability to Discuss Issues

When Pope John Paul II issued his Apostolic Letter *Ordinatio Sacerdotalis* in May 1994, few people were surprised when he took the position that 'women are not to be admitted to ordination'.[3] In his previous sixteen years as Pope, John Paul had done little to suggest he was in favour of women participating more fully in the life of the Church. What did come as a surprise, however, was the Pope's statement that the issue was no longer open to debate, but must be 'definitely held by all the Church's faithful'. This declaration was greeted with both dismay and disbelief. How could a question about who can exercise various ministries in the Church be closed off from discussion? One could understand such an approach in the area of basic Church doctrine, but questions about the Church's ministries have been evolving throughout its history.

In any case, as happens in these situations, the pope's statement only served to stimulate more discussion on the issue. Indeed, the question of whether or not women should have equal participation in the Catholic Church, along with men, will simply not go away, and attempts to shut down discussion on the matter will not resolve anything.

Of course, it is not only the matter of women's participation in the Church that the Pope, and the bishops, find difficult to discuss. There are many other issues that the laity want to talk about, and the hierarchy are hesitant to do so. The question of contraception is another example.

In 1968 Pope Paul VI published an encyclical entitled Humane Vitae, which stated that 'each and every marital act must of necessity retain its intrinsic relationship to the procreation of human life'.[4] In other words, any form of artificial contraception is forbidden, under any circumstances. The Pope based his decision on the natural law argument that while not every act of intercourse results in conception, the unitive and procreative aspects of the marriage act cannot be separated.

This statement came out fifty years ago, and yet in all that time there has never been any attempt to look at the question again. In the 1980s, when the AIDS epidemic took hold, particularly in Africa, a few bishops dared to suggest that the use of condoms, forbidden by the Pope, may not be a worse thing than the deaths of millions of people from the AIDS virus. Unfortunately, their pleas fell on deaf ears. There was to be no review of Humane Vitae.

---

3. *Ordinatio Sacerdotalis* (*Priestly Ordination* in English), promulgated by Pope John Paul II on 22 May 1994, the Vatican, paragraph 4.
4. *Humanae Vitae* promulgated by Pope Paul VI on 25 July 1968, St Peter's, Rome, paragraph 11.

The inability of the Church hierarchy to discuss questions they find uncomfortable is not only restricted to theological issues. At the personal level, too, many bishops have difficulty dealing with matters they find awkward. The common response is simply to ignore the issue, and hope it will go away.

Over the past thirty years as a priest in my archdiocese, I have written only four personal letters to the particular bishops of the day. The letters were written very respectfully and affably. The topics of those letters were not overly important. I simply wanted to express my views at the time, and I felt the bishop was the appropriate person to hear what I had to say. I do admit that some of those issues were a little contentious.

In any case, I didn't receive a reply to any of those four letters, which at the beginning I found rather strange. I couldn't imagine myself, as parish priest, for example, receiving a letter from a parishioner and not responding to it, no matter what the letter was about, or who the parishioner was. But by the time I sent the fourth letter, more than twenty years after the first, I was no longer expecting a reply. I could see that it was just going to be too difficult for the bishop to deal with.

Finding it difficult to enter into discussion with those who may hold different views to yourself, and even just not exchanging the normal courtesies of life such as replying to letters, is not uncommon among the clergy. I think it may come from the fact that bishops and priests rarely have to justify anything they do. Bishops can make sweeping changes to their dioceses without having to get the agreement of anyone else. All the committees they sit on are advisory committees only, as is the case with parish priests. The parish priest can disband the parish council any time he wishes, and make all the decisions about the parish himself.

When there is no accountability, no checks and balances, it is easy to see how priests and bishops can develop an attitude that they do not have to engage in any dialogue they might find uncomfortable. They only have to respond to those they wish to, and in so many cases, any issue they find challenging can simply be ignored. It is an attitude that develops out of the club mentality, while at the same time it works to reinforce it.

Overseas Clergy

One of the policies that has had a big effect on the local Church in Sydney is the decision by the bishops to invite priests from the developing countries to come and work in the Sydney Archdiocese. I can understand the position that the bishops found themselves in. Vocations to the priesthood declined rapidly in the 1980s, and have never really recovered. The bishops could see that there would be a long-term scarcity of priests in the archdiocese, and so looked to places like India, Africa and the Philippines, where there seemed to be an almost endless supply of vocations to the priesthood and religious life. Priests from these countries were happy to come and work in Sydney, and now make up a sizable percentage of the archdiocesan clergy.

The first point I want to make about the issue is that, given the huge impact this policy was to have on the archdiocese, there should have been some sort of consultation process with both the local priests and the laity before the decision was made. Certainly, the scarcity of priests was a serious problem and needed to be addressed. But it was a problem for the whole Sydney Church, not just for the bishops, and the whole Sydney Church should have been involved in dealing with the problem, and working out appropriate ways to resolve it.

Even after the decision was made there should have been a process put in place in the archdiocese to assist the laity in learning about the cultures, and particularly the religious cultures, of the countries where the priests were coming from. It would have been very helpful in enabling the parishioners to understand something of the mentality and the background of the new priests, and it would have also made it easier for the priests themselves to settle into their new religious environment.

I must say my own personal experience of living and working with priests from overseas has been very positive. In my last parish, over a thirteen-year period, there were five priests from non-English speaking countries who worked in the parish as assistant priests. We all worked well together, and had a lot of fun at the same time. Over that thirteen-year period I did not have one cross word with any of them, or them with me.

Nevertheless, it cannot be denied that the policy of inviting priests from developing countries to work in the Sydney Church has brought with it some challenging issues. The first relates to language and communication.

I am the first to admit how difficult it is to minister as a priest in a language that is not your mother tongue. When I was studying in Rome I used to help out regularly in a parish, mainly celebrating Sunday Masses. One year I looked after the parish for a month while the parish priest was away on annual holidays. I did my very best to communicate with the parishioners, whether I was celebrating a funeral, or just sitting around at a parish social event. But I was constantly struggling with the language, and my ministry was not anywhere near as effective as it was in Australia. There are only so many times you can say 'I beg your pardon', before you start to nod knowingly, and slip out of the conversation. It is particularly difficult in a group setting, or at meetings, when comments are flying back and forth in rapid succession. This explains why some priests from overseas, who are quite capable of communicating on a one to one basis, often have little to say in parish meetings or in social groups.

It is not just the priest himself who is struggling, but also the parishioners, when they are listening to a Sunday homily being delivered by a priest with poor English skills. In some cases the priest has a reasonable command of the language, but his accent is so strong that it is very difficult to understand what he is actually saying. I know that some priests in this situation put their homilies up on the screen in the church, or have printed sheets available for the parishioners, which I am sure provides some help, but clearly this arrangement is less than satisfactory.

The other issue relates to culture, and in particular the differences between the culture of the overseas priest and that of his new homeland. While Australia incorporates a mix of many different ethnic groups, there is still an identifiable Australian culture that is underpinned by values such as egalitarianism and a sense of the 'fair go'. It is also a secular culture, and while religion plays an important role in the life of many Australians, there is a clear separation of Church and State.

Some of the overseas priests come from a very different culture, and find the Australian religious culture quite unfamiliar. One priest told me that when he came to work in Sydney, one of the things that struck him was the fact that the Sunday Mass collections are often counted by the parishioners. He said that in his own diocese back home this would never happen. Only the parish priest would ever count the money, and if he had to get some assistance he would get his family in to help. This may seem only a small matter, but it says a lot about things like lay ministry and transparency, things that this particular priest had to get used to in Australia.

Some priests come from countries where women do not have the same rights as men. Priests from these countries may not be used to working with women in professional roles, particularly within the Church. When this is combined with a culture that is based on a class structure, and where the priest is at the top of the tree, it can be very confusing for the new priest, and not always easy for him to work out the appropriate way of relating.

I do not mention these things to be critical or negative. I mention them because they are real issues experienced by both the overseas priests and the people in the parishes where they work, and yet the bishops refuse to acknowledge it. In the many years that priests have been coming to work in the diocese from overseas I have never heard the topic discussed at a clergy conference. No bishop has ever suggested that there may be some problems that need to be addressed. The attitude of the bishops seems to be that it doesn't really matter whether the parishioners can understand the priest or not. He is still saying a valid Mass, and the parishioners have fulfilled their Sunday obligation.

Surely this is another example of the disconnect between the clergy and the laity, because in reality, it does indeed matter whether the congregation is able to understand the priest at Mass.

Vatican II

The Second Vatican Council had an enormous impact on the life of the Church, and in particular, on the role of the laity, and the laity's relationship with the clergy. Prior to the Council, ministry in the Church was seen, by and large, as the domain of the clergy. The laity did not play an active role in the liturgy, or for the most part, in other parish ministries. Of course, there were areas in the parish where they could assist, but it was seen more as 'helping Father'.

That all changed with Vatican II. As the official documents emanating from Rome were being read and reflected on, it soon became clear that the laity were being recognised as having ministries in their own right, and were to have a much more active role in the life of the Church. Men and women began taking on roles such as reader, acolyte and catechist. Parish councils were being formed, along with liturgy committees, finance committees, and a whole host of parish groups and lay associations.

Understandably, these changes were not always easy for the clergy to accept. The laity were now doing some things that the priests had traditionally done, and they were even becoming involved in decision-making processes within the new parish structures. For the first time, priests and bishops were being challenged to rethink their relationship with the laity. This involved not only putting new emphasis on the role of lay ministry, but also looking at new ways of exercising their own priestly ministry.

Perhaps the most obvious sign of the new recognition given to the laity in the Church came with the changes to the Mass liturgy. Having the Mass said in the language of the people, rather than in Latin, which was the language of the clergy, sent a powerful message that 'full and active participation by all the people is the aim to be considered before all else'.[5] In a similar way, when the priest turned around and faced the people to say Mass, it reminded everyone that the Mass is a celebration by the whole community, gathered around the altar together.

It is interesting that some priests are still finding these changes difficult to accept. There are even some priests, not born at the time of the Vatican Council, who prefer saying Mass in Latin, and having their backs to the people. I know they are coming from a different perspective to myself on the issue, but I find it difficult to understand why they would not want to share, in the fullest way possible, the celebration of the Mass with the whole congregation.

The Vatican Council will continue to be, I am sure, a controversial issue, particularly among the clergy. Some bishops and priests will always feel that changes brought about by the Council took away from the solemnity and mystique that characterised the Church up to that time. Others will see the changes as bringing a new openness and vitality to the Church. But one thing is clear - the laity themselves do not want to go back to a model of Church where they can no longer participate in a full and active way.

---

5. Constitution on the Sacred Liturgy, *Sacrosanctum Concilium* promulgated by Pope Paul VI, 4 December, 1968, paragraph 14.

CASE STUDY – Gluten-free Altar Breads

So far in this section I have looked at many different ways that the clergy club mentality expresses itself in the Church. I have not gone into detail about any particular aspect, preferring to give a general overview of the topic. I would now like to take a specific issue, that of the gluten-free altar bread, and study it a little more thoroughly, and in the process, show how a number of the various facets of clericalism can come together in a single issue. I have chosen this particular topic for the case study because it is a very real question that is affecting more and more Catholics every year.

The gluten question basically comes down to this dilemma. On the one hand, the Church hierarchy insists that only bread made from wheat or wheaten derivatives, and thus containing gluten, can be used at Mass, while on the other hand, people who suffer from coeliac disease cannot tolerate bread containing gluten. It presents a real conundrum, and both the Church hierarchy and those with coeliac disease have strong arguments supporting their respective cases.

So, what exactly is gluten?

Gluten is a family of proteins found in cereal grains such as wheat, rye and barley. It has a glue-like property that gives the elastic texture to dough which assists in the making of bread.

What are the health issues around gluten?

Most people can tolerate gluten, but for those who suffer from coeliac disease, or even for those with gluten sensitivity or wheat allergy, it can cause a range of problems including abdominal pain, cramping, tissue damage to the gut, headaches and tiredness.

What is the relevance of gluten to the sacrament of Holy Communion?

The debate around gluten has brought up questions around the kind of bread that can be used at Mass. The bishops argue that the bread needs to be, what might be termed, 'real' bread, and it can only be 'real' bread if it contains wheat, or a wheaten derivative. Thus, breads made from wheat, barley or rye are suitable for use at Mass, but a bread made from maize, for example, which contains no wheat, is not permitted.

At the heart of the problem is that gluten is found in all wheat-based products, and therefore all breads that are permitted to be used at Mass will contain some gluten. Thus, people with coeliac disease are not able to come and receive Communion, at least in the same way that the rest of the congregation does.

Historical background

Before 2003 no one really gave much attention to the use of gluten free altar breads. They were being produced by Catholic distributors, along with the regular altar breads. The gluten-free breads were being made from maize cornflour. In the parish where I was at the time, we received a regular supply of gluten-free altar breads which were consecrated at Mass and given to people with coeliac disease or gluten allergies, on request.

The situation changed dramatically when, on 24 July 2003, the Congregation for the Faith in Rome put out an instruction which said, in part, 'Hosts that are completely gluten-free are invalid matter for the celebration of the Eucharist. Low-gluten hosts (partially gluten-free) are valid matter, provided they contain a sufficient amount of gluten to obtain the confection of bread without the addition of foreign materials and without the use of procedures that would alter the nature of bread'.[6] When the instruction was received by the Australian National Liturgical Commission they informed the Catholic distributors that they were to cease making gluten-free altar breads.

Low-gluten altar breads

One of the ways that the bishops have tried to respond to the problem is by allowing the use of low-gluten altar breads, with a gluten content around 200 parts per million. This is a workable solution for those with a gluten allergy that is not severe. But for the coeliac sufferers even the tiniest amount of gluten can cause symptoms to appear.

Receiving from the chalice

Another way that the bishops have attempted to deal with the problem is to suggest that people with coeliac disease should receive only the consecrated wine, thereby avoiding the gluten problem with the bread. There are two issues that come up with this suggestion. First, it is very unusual for people to receive Communion without receiving

---

6. Congregation for the Faith, Vatican City, Letter to Presidents of Episcopal Conferences (Prot. 89/78 – 17498), 24 July, 2003.

the consecrated bread. Many parishes do not provide the consecrated wine, but no parish would ever offer Communion without offering the consecrated bread. Thus, the bishops are asking coeliac sufferers to do something that has never been part of the Catholic way of receiving Holy Communion.

The other problem is a logistical one. Those who cannot receive a gluten host would have to come to the sanctuary and receive from the chalice, perhaps while Communion was being given to the ministers. Many people would not want to go up to the sanctuary and receive Communion in such a public way. They may not want everyone in the congregation to know about their health issue. Children, in particular, may not want to be singled out from their peers in such a way.

There is also the question about consuming alcohol. For various reasons, some people do not wish to consume alcohol, under any circumstances, and others may not want their children consuming alcohol, especially at a very young age.

Clearly there are many aspects to this question. To me, it is a classic case of the clergy club mentality in action. With this in mind I would like to now look at some of the ways I feel the bishops' response to the gluten-free issue is in keeping with the way the clergy club works.

Lack of consultation
The decision to ban gluten-free altar breads was made at the Vatican level. I have no information as to whether any consultation took place before the decision was made, but if there was any consultation I certainly have not heard or read anything about it here.

What is clear, however, is that once the decision was received by the local Church in Sydney, there was no process of consultation as to how the policy would be implemented, or what might be some of the potential problems needing to be addressed.

The first we knew about it at the parish level was when we received correspondence informing us of the decision that had been made, and the fact that gluten-free altar breads were no longer to be used at Mass. I remember having to tell one of our parishioners who suffered from a severe gluten allergy about the decision. She was deeply distressed.

Surely if the bishops had listened to people in the parishes who suffer from coeliac disease and wheat allergies they would have had a far better understanding of the issues involved, and would have been in a much better position to implement the policy effectively and with sensitivity.

Legalism

The gluten-free debate highlights two issues that are often in tension within the Church—the application of the law, and the pastoral care of the people. No one is denying that there is a legal aspect to this question. The Roman instruction has made it very clear that gluten-free altar breads are forbidden. That is now Church law. At the same time it cannot be denied that there is an important pastoral issue at stake here, the participation of the faithful in the Eucharist at Mass. The question surely must be asked, 'Which is more important?'

The bishops have made it clear that observing the law is their first priority. At the time the issue was being debated, a member of the Australian National Liturgical Commission, speaking on behalf of the Commission, said, 'I am trying to find a solution that will satisfy the instruction but that will also enable Catholics with coeliac disease to participate in the sacramental life of the Church.'[7] Certainly from the way that statement is constructed, it is obvious that satisfying the legal instruction is the first priority, and the people's participation in the Eucharist is the second.

I am not in any way suggesting that the bishops don't have pastoral concern for the people in their care. I am sure they wish this situation had never arisen. In fact, they often look somewhat uncomfortable when defending their position on gluten-free altar breads. But defend it they do. The law must be observed, but once that is done, they are then prepared to do whatever they can to help the parishioners who have these health issues.

Appeal to doctrine

Around the time the decision came out, I was discussing the issue with one of the bishops. He was saying that using wheat, and thus gluten, in the bread for Mass was an issue of Church doctrine. I respectfully disagreed. 'How can an issue about the ingredients of the bread at Mass be a doctrinal matter', I asked. He responded with, 'Well, it's at the lower end of the scale'.

People may argue about whether the gluten-free issue is actually on the doctrinal scale at all, although certainly for that bishop it was.

---

7. Executive Officer of the Australian National Liturgical Commission in interview with *Online Catholics* Article entitled 'Valid' Hosts Could Make You Sick', 18 August, 2004.

What concerns me, however, is the attitude that if something can be described as 'doctrine', even at the low end of the scale, then it is fixed and unchangeable, and there is no point discussing the matter further.

An appeal to doctrine should not be used as an excuse to avoid tackling important contemporary issues, no matter how difficult they may be. We are constantly improving our scientific knowledge, particularly with regard to medical science. We know far more about health issues such as allergies than we ever did in the past. Questions about gluten had never arisen in the past, because until recently we were unaware of its effect on the human body.

The other question that has to be asked is, 'How do you determine what is "real" bread, and what is "not real" bread?' On what basis do the bishops say that gluten-free bread is 'not real' bread? The relevant Vatican instruction states that the bread used at Mass must be made 'purely from wheat' and cannot be bread made from another grain. Presumably, then, only bread made from wheat is 'real bread', but, to me, this seems to be a very subjective judgement.

The question of exceptions

One of the characteristics of much of the Church's teaching is that it does not allow for exceptions to the rule. A position is either right or wrong, and if it is right, then it is right in every case, and if it is wrong, then it is wrong in every case. This is because the bishops tend to use an objective, deductive approach to problem solving, and don't put a lot of emphasis on the subjective or practical dimensions of an issue. The gluten-free question is a typical example.

But life is not like that. We live in a world that is constantly making exceptions, according to the need or the urgency of the situation. We have speed limits on our roads, for example, for good reason, but if a fire crew is trying to get to a serious house fire, it is permissible for the driver of the fire engine to exceed the speed limit. This does not mean that the driver has no respect for the road rules. It simply means that there are times when an exception has to be made, an exception that in no way undermines the importance of the general rule.

The question around altar breads at Mass cries out for an exception to be made for people who cannot tolerate gluten. The exception would not in any way undermine the basic guideline that the bread used at Mass should be made from wheat. It simply underlines the complexity and problematic nature of so many of life's issues, including this one.

If only everything was clear-cut and simple. But in the real world it is anything but. Doubt and ambiguity are found everywhere in life, and we must be very careful about applying simplistic solutions to complicated problems.

The issue of coeliac sufferers receiving Holy Communion is a complex problem, and has to be dealt with on many levels. A simple recourse to a Vatican statement about bread having to be made from wheat is far too simplistic. The pastoral concerns are at least as relevant as the ingredients of the bread, and should be given the same importance in the discussion.

Final note

In June 2017, the Vatican Congregation for Divine Worship and the Discipline of the Sacraments published a document on the gluten-free issue. It is entitled 'Circular letter to Bishops on the bread and wine for the Eucharist'. Once again, the Congregation states that 'Hosts that are completely gluten-free are invalid matter for the celebration of the Eucharist'.[8]

The thing that strikes me about the document, and indeed saddens me, is that nowhere in the letter is there any mention of the people with gluten allergies. It's as if they don't exist. The only people who are mentioned are the bishops and priests who have to follow the ruling, and 'those who prepare these materials', the people who make the altar breads. Could it be that the bishops are so concerned about the ingredients of the bread, that they cannot see the people who come to receive it?

Conclusion to Part 3

In this section I have looked at different ways that the clergy club mentality expresses itself in the life of the Church. The examples I have used are many and varied, and this is because the clergy club mentality finds its way into almost every aspect of the Church's life.

In the next section I want to look at Jesus and the Gospels. I want to look at his leadership, his world view, his way of ministering, and his life generally, and present it as a model for leadership in our contemporary Church.

---

8. Congregation for Divine Worship and the Discipline of the Sacraments, Circular Letter to Bishops on the Bread and Wine for the Eucharist, Prot. N. 320/17, 15 June, 2017, paragraph 4.

Part 4
Jesus, the Gospel, and the Clergy Club

The Compass

In the first three parts of this book I have looked at many different aspects of clericalism, and have made no secret of the fact that I believe it is a very real and current phenomenon in the Catholic Church. I have also made no secret of the fact that I think the attitude behind clericalism, what I call the clergy club mentality, is hurting the Church, particularly in the way it is causing tension and disconnection between the clergy and the laity. I am also quite open about the fact that I believe things need to change.

But how do I know that I am on the right track? How do I know that things need to change? Could it be that the clergy club mentality is a normal and appropriate attitude for ordained ministers in the Church? Could it be that clericalism is just a natural expression of priesthood? I am sure there would be some people reading this book, and many who will never read this book, who would feel that the clergy are indeed 'special' among the members of the Church, and do deserve to be treated with more reverence and respect than others. But once again I ask, how do we know?

The answer lies in the person of Jesus, in his life, in his teachings, in what he said, and in what he did. Jesus is the compass point, by which we, as his witnesses, measure our life journey. If we want to know what priesthood looks like, indeed if we want to know what any Christian ministry looks like, then we need look no further than the life of the man from Nazareth. He is the model by which we compare our own lives, our own actions, and our own behaviour. That's what it means to be Christian. Indeed, the Christian life, surely, is about trying to constantly conform our own lives, and our own attitudes, to those of

Christ. St Paul puts it very succinctly in his first letter to the Corinthians when he speaks of having 'the mind of Christ' (1 Cor 2:16).

It's the same for all members of the Church, parishioners and popes. As Christians, trying to make good decisions about how to live our day to day lives, we look at our actions and say, 'Is this the sort of thing we could see Jesus doing, given what we know of him?' So too, for the hierarchy, trying to make good decisions about how to lead the Church. They do exactly the same thing, asking the question, 'Is this the sort of thing we could see Jesus doing, given what we know of him?' Ultimately, it is the only criterion necessary to ensure that the Church we have today is the Church that Jesus wants.

We are so fortunate to have the four accounts of the Gospel, which give us so many insights into the person of Jesus, and lets us see 'the mind of Christ' in action. We see him relating to a whole range of people, including Jews and Gentiles, friends and strangers, soldiers and tax collectors, people in authority and people stricken with terrible diseases. We also see Jesus in a whole variety of situations. Some cause him tension. Some cause him sadness. Some are joy filled, and some are extremely painful. And through it all, Jesus consistently expresses who he is, in both his divinity and his humanity.

Let us now look at some of those people that Jesus encounters, and some of those situations that he experiences, as described by the Gospel writers. Let us see how Jesus thinks, what his attitudes are, what sort of decisions he makes, and how he acts. In particular, let us see if there are any traces of a club mentality in the way he sees the world.

Like all of us, Jesus is consistent in his thinking, and his behaviour. And it is that consistency, those common themes running through his life, that are the real insights into who he is, and who we should be.

'I Have Come to Bring Good News to the Poor' (Lk 4: 16–21)

At the beginning of Jesus' public ministry, when he had returned to his home town of Nazareth, he went to the synagogue and read aloud a passage from the prophet Isaiah. Jesus could have chosen any section from the prophet's writings, but the passage he deliberately chose, and clearly wanted the people to hear, was the following: 'The Spirit of the Lord is upon me, because he has anointed me to bring good news to the poor. He has sent me to proclaim release to the captives and recovery of sight to the blind, to let the oppressed go free, to proclaim the year of the Lord's favour' (Lk 4:18).

When Jesus had finished reading the passage Luke tells us that he sat down, and with the eyes of all in the synagogue fixed on him, he said, 'Today this scripture has been fulfilled in your hearing' (Lk 4:21).

Clearly, Jesus saw the words of Isaiah as saying a lot about his own life and his own ministry. They are words about joy, freedom and forgiveness. Jesus saw his message as good news, not bad news. And it was particularly directed towards the marginalised, especially those who were poor, those who were oppressed, and those who could not see. His proclaiming of the 'year of the Lord's favour' has particular significance as it referred to a year, recurring every fifty years, when slaves and prisoners were freed, debts were cancelled, and a special emphasis was placed on forgiveness.

All these themes were fundamental to Jesus' teaching, and his actions. He sought out the poor, the sick, the blind, and those who in any way had lost their freedom and dignity. This was his starting point, the basis of everything else that was to come.

For the clergy, it is a blueprint for ministry. If we, as priests and bishops, do not seek out the people that Jesus sought out, support the oppressed as Jesus supported them, forgive as Jesus forgave, bring freedom as Jesus brought freedom, then our ministry is not valid Christian ministry. We may be still bringing a message, but it is not the message of Jesus.

It is interesting that this particular passage from Luke figures prominently in the liturgy for the Holy Week Chrism Mass. Taking place traditionally on Holy Thursday morning, the Chrism Mass is celebrated in the diocesan cathedral, with the bishops and priests from the diocese coming together to celebrate, among other things, a renewal of their ordination promises. The Gospel reading is the passage quoted above, while the first reading contains the original words from the prophet Isaiah. What appropriate readings for a celebration of priesthood! And yet the curious thing is that rarely have I heard a bishop actually preach on these readings at a Chrism Mass. Instead, they tend to share something of their own perspective on priesthood.

I would love to see Pope Francis challenge all bishops around the world to preach on these readings at their next Chrism Mass.

'Why Does Your Teacher Eat with Tax Collectors and Sinners' (Mt 9:11)

Jesus was often criticised for the company he kept. In particular, he was criticised by the Pharisees for having meals with tax collectors and sinners. The tax collectors were a particularly despised group. They were Jews themselves, collecting taxes for the Romans from their own Jewish people, and thus seen as traitors. The sinners were seen as immoral and irreligious, and certainly not the sort of people that a religious preacher like Jesus would be expected to associate with.

So why did Jesus share their company? Certainly, he was trying to show them a more noble and dignified way of life, as evidenced by his comment that it is not the healthy who need the doctor, but the sick. But it is more than this. He makes no demands on them, and he clearly enjoys their friendship. They were all people with individual stories, most likely trying to do the best they could with what they had. And Jesus loved them for it.

All ministry is based on love, not just a cerebral 'love your enemies' type of attitude, but a love that engages people in such a way that you have no enemies, you make no distinctions between saints and sinners. They are all just people, doing their best.

The clergy must be particularly careful to treat everyone the same. In parish ministry, there is always a temptation for us priests to cultivate special friendships with families and individuals with whom we may feel more at home. Perhaps they are more involved in the life of the parish than others. Perhaps they contribute financially in a very generous way. Or maybe we just enjoy their conversation and hospitality.

Of course, there is nothing wrong with that, as long as we spend the same amount of time with those who may have more needs, who may be more demanding, who we don't feel quite as comfortable with, who may not be involved in any parish groups or activities, or who may contribute little to the parish finances.

I always feel that a good litmus test for the way people respond to the needs of others, in terms of how selective or non-selective they are, is the way they deal with phone messages. It is particularly true for the clergy. In a busy parish office the phone rings constantly. Many of the calls are dealt with by the parish staff, but some people need to speak directly to the priest. It is not unusual to come in from a funeral, for example, and have five or six people to call back. Some you know, some you don't. Some requests can be easily fixed up, others are far more complicated and time consuming. The temptation is to deal with the easy ones, and leave the hard ones on the back burner. But we all know that Jesus wouldn't do that.

The clergy can be selective in other ways too. Once when I was in Italy, I noticed a sign outside a church stating that men wearing shorts or women wearing sleeveless dresses were not to enter the church. These types of signs of course, are not uncommon. I can understand why the clergy would not want people entering the church wearing vulgar or obscene dress, but here we are talking about normal summer clothing that would be generally accepted around the world. I couldn't help but think, 'Would the same Jesus who ate with sinners and tax collectors not want to eat with women wearing sleeveless dresses and men wearing shorts?'

'What Were You Arguing about on the Way?' (Mk 9:33)

Jesus was constantly getting frustrated with his disciples. No matter how many times he spoke to them about the importance of humility and service, they just didn't get the message. On this occasion, they are walking together towards Capernaum, and obviously along the road Jesus hears some of them arguing among themselves. When they arrive at Capernaum Jesus asks them what they have been arguing about on the way. The disciples are embarrassed, and say nothing. In fact, they have been arguing among themselves about who is the greatest.

Jesus is not impressed. He sits down, calls the disciples over, and reminds them once again that God's idea of greatness is very different to what was generally accepted then, and now. 'Whoever wants to be first', he says to them, 'must be last of all, and servant of all'.

Most people want to be successful in life and achieve as much as they can. It is just part of being human. Particularly in one's career, there is a desire to get on, and move up the ladder. We do not know what prompted the disciples' discussion about who was the greatest. Perhaps they were talking about who might take over as leader of the group when Jesus was gone.

By and large, priests are no different to anyone else in wanting to move up the ladder and take on more responsibility. There is nothing wrong in wanting to further one's career. The clergy, however, have to be particularly careful, because in the Church there are not the normal checks and balances you find in most institutions. Priests are appointed to positions by the bishop. Bishops are appointed to positions by the pope. There are no interviews, no curriculum vitae. There are no job descriptions. There is no set of objective criteria on which decisions are based. And because it is all subjective, it's easy to see how there could be a real temptation among both priests and bishops to 'impress the boss'.

'Is it Lawful to Do Good or to Do Harm on the Sabbath?' (Mk 3:4)

There are numerous accounts in the gospels of Jesus breaking the Sabbath laws. It's almost as if he goes out of his way to do it. On this occasion Mark tells us that Jesus cures a man with a withered hand, something that would have been prohibited on the Sabbath. The Pharisees are watching him carefully, ready to accuse him of breaking one of their most important religious laws. But Jesus speaks first. 'Is it lawful to do good or to do harm on the Sabbath', he says, 'to save life or to kill?'

Jesus' attitude to religious law is a very interesting one. He certainly has respect for the law. On one occasion he says, 'Do not think that I have come to abolish the law or the prophets; I have come not to abolish but to fulfil' (Mt 5:17). And yet he so regularly, and blatantly, breaks the law for a higher good. Clearly, for Jesus the law is not an end in itself. It has its purpose, but if law gets in the way of what is good and life-giving, then it must be ignored. As he so succinctly puts it on another occasion, 'The Sabbath was made for humankind, and not humankind for the Sabbath' (Mk 2:27).

Religious law, or canon law as it is called, will always have its place in the life of the Church. There needs to be some codifying of our rituals, policies and practices to ensure consistency and order in what we believe, and how we express ourselves as Church. But it is crucial that those who formulate the Church's laws keep in mind Jesus' own attitude to law, and never allow it to become an end in itself.

'We Tried to Stop Him' (Mk 9:38)

How wrong we can all be at times, even with the best will in the world.

John, the youngest disciple, finds this out one day when he is telling Jesus that he and a number of the other disciples had come across someone casting out demons in Jesus' name, and they tried to stop him because he was not one of their group. I'm sure John was anticipating a positive response from Jesus, but the reply he got was the exact opposite. 'Do not stop him', says Jesus, 'whoever is not against us is for us'.

It is usually a lot easier to say 'no', than to say 'yes'. 'No' keeps the status quo. 'No' is safe. When we stop someone from doing something, or stop initiatives from taking place, we stay in control and feel secure.

I believe one of the great mistakes that has been made by the Church hierarchy in recent times is the banning of the Third Rite of Reconciliation. Admittedly, this particular form of the sacrament, with general absolution rather than individual absolution, was originally designed for exceptional circumstances, when it is logistically impossible to hear all the confessions individually. But circumstances change, and during the 1990s in particular, the Third Rite became quite widespread and extremely popular, at least throughout the Sydney Archdiocese. Churches were packed with parishioners of all ages coming to the sacrament of Reconciliation, especially during Lent and Advent. By any measure, the Third Rite was one of the most successful initiatives in the Church over the past fifty years, and the bishops stopped it.

The argument from the hierarchy was that under normal circumstances absolution could only be given if the penitents actually verbalised their sins to the priest. I am not sure where this concept comes from. It is certainly not based in Scripture. I can't think of many cases, if any, where anyone actually confesses their sins to Jesus before they are forgiven. In fact, in the parable of the prodigal son, which is the classic story of God's forgiveness, when the son returns home to his father and begins to tell his story, the father cuts him off, and orders the feast to be prepared. Sorrow is all that matters, even imperfect sorrow, and that sorrow is expressed in the fact that the son came back (Lk 15:11–32).

But whatever one's position on the theology or the form of the sacrament of Reconciliation, surely the fact that so many people were once again coming to the sacrament, should have prompted the response, 'Let's not stop them'.

'Zacchaeus, Hurry and Come Down' (Lk 19:5)

One of my favourite Gospel passages is the story of the tax collector Zacchaeus, the man who climbed a tree to get a better look at Jesus as he passed by. Zacchaeus is certainly an engaging character with his unorthodox and somewhat comical attempt to encounter Jesus. But it is not so much Zacchaeus' desire to get a better look at Jesus that captures my imagination, but rather Jesus' desire to get a better look at Zacchaeus.

The story could easily have ended with Jesus noticing Zacchaeus in the tree and acknowledging his efforts and ingenuity. That was all that Zacchaeus would have expected, and Jesus did not need to do any more. But Jesus was never about doing only what was required. He loved people, and he loved their stories, and he loved being part of their stories. He clearly loved Zacchaeus, and he wanted to be part of his story. 'Come down', he said to him, 'I must stay at your house today'.

One of the basic requirements for priesthood is to have a genuine love for people, to be interested in their stories, and to want to be part of their stories. Unfortunately, some of the clergy struggle to express these qualities in their ministry. They sometimes appear to act out of a sense of duty, without any great enthusiasm or passion. They will do what needs to be done, but find it difficult going the extra mile. Many parishioners have commented that they feel they are disturbing Father when they approach him about a particular issue. Some feel anxious about even calling him, in case they catch him at a bad time.

Certainly, there are time constraints on what the priest can do, but it is the attitude that is important. By the way the clergy act towards their parishioners they are saying one of two things, 'Do not worry me unless it's important', or 'Come down, I must stay at your house today'

'Which of These Three, Do You Think, Was a Neighbour' Lk 10:36

The parable of the Good Samaritan is one of the best known of all Jesus parables. It is a simple story about a man who is robbed and beaten, and left to die at the side of the road, and how three people, the priest, the Levite and the Samaritan, walk down the road, see the man, and then make decisions about how they will respond, or not respond.

One of the temptations when looking at Jesus' parables is to make heroes of some people, and villains of others. It satisfies our desire to find neat solutions to complex issues. But life is not so straightforward. Yes, there are some people that we might describe as heroes, and there are some we might call villains, but most of us are somewhere in between, perhaps heroes one day and villains the next.

In the parable of the Good Samaritan the temptation is to find one hero, the Samaritan, and two villains, the priest and the Levite, but that is not necessarily the case. All three were making decisions that they thought were the right ones. The priest and the Levite were trying to weigh up two competing demands. On the one hand, they were faced with the immediate situation of a man lying on the side of the road, needing help. They knew they had an obligation to assist if they could. On the other hand, they were bound by the purification rules associated with their religious positions. Both the priest and the Levite were temple officials, the priest offering sacrifice, among other things, and the Levite assisting in the temple worship. They knew that if they touched the blood of the injured man they would be rendered impure, and not be able to carry out their roles in the temple without long and complex cleansing rituals. Faced with this dilemma, they chose to obey the purification laws, which, in their minds at least, justified their decision not to stop and care for the injured man.

The Samaritan, however, was not faced with any such dilemma. He was not restrained by any religious laws or practices that could compromise his decision to help the man in need. He was free to respond as a 'neighbour' should, and he did exactly that.

The parable is full of meaning on many levels, but there is certainly a message there for the clergy, not to get so caught up in the laws and traditions of the Church, that the real issue, the duty to respond to people's needs in a caring and loving way, becomes almost secondary.

I have already mentioned issues such as the ban on gluten free altar breads, and the exclusion of women from reader and acolyte institution ceremonies. These types of issues, I believe, fall into this category, where law and tradition become more important than people, and their needs and hopes.

'They Have No Wine' Jn 2:3

Jesus expressed many fine human qualities in his life but one that perhaps we don't think about often is the fact that he was a good listener. We see this quality particularly evident in the story of the wedding feast of Cana.

Jesus has been invited to the wedding, along with his mother and his disciples. During the meal the wine runs out. Mary is the first to notice and says to Jesus, 'They have no wine'. She does not say any more than that. She does not ask Jesus to do anything about it. She simply says, 'They have no wine'.

At first Jesus is reluctant to act, but eventually he does, obviously thinking not only about what his mother said, but why she said it. As Jesus so often did, he was not only listening to the words, but also to what was behind the words.

Listening is so important in all relationships. When we are really prepared to listen to someone, we are saying, 'Your thoughts are important', 'Your ideas deserve consideration', 'You matter'.

It is always important for those in leadership positions to be good listeners. It is particularly important for the clergy to listen to the laity.

Unfortunately, however, because of the structure of the Church, it is not easy for the laity to have their voice heard. There are few avenues of genuine communication, and as a consequence the laity are often hesitant to raise their concerns or even just express their thoughts directly to the clergy. And so, priests and bishops need to take the initiative, to try and understand how the laity feel, to listen carefully to their words, and to what lies behind the words.

I would like to take one example where I believe the hierarchy have been very slow to listen to what the people are saying, and have been saying for decades. It relates particularly to the youth in our Church, and how they see the Mass.

One of the constant comments that young people make about the Mass is that 'the Mass is boring'. It was said fifty years ago when I was a teenager, and it is still being said today. Certainly, much is done at the parish level to try to make the Sunday celebration of the Mass engaging and relevant, but ultimately the structure is fixed, and there is little scope for creativity and imagination.

Of course, it could be argued that people who say the Mass is boring don't really understand the Mass. They are simply looking at it from a superficial viewpoint and fail to reflect on the profound meaning of the prayers and readings and actions that make the Mass what it is. That may be so, although I know of many people who have a deep appreciation of the Mass liturgy, but still find it boring.

In any case, it is futile to expect the majority of young people to have a developed sense of the theological significance of the Mass. They work at the experiential level. They walk into a church and see rows of pews. They listen to readings that were written thousands of years ago which they find difficult to understand, and which often mean very little to them. They hear prayers that are written in stilted language and include words they never hear, and never use. They have little chance to express themselves in the liturgy, apart from participating in the standard Mass responses. It is no wonder they find it boring, and have been saying so for years.

This is where it is necessary for the hierarchy to enter into genuine dialogue with our young people about how to celebrate the Sunday liturgy. There also needs to be more reflection on questions such as 'Is there some room for flexibility in the way the Mass is celebrated?' 'How can we engage young people more fully in the celebration of the Mass?' 'What suggestions do our young people have about making the Mass a more meaningful celebration for them?'

Perhaps in the end nothing will change. Perhaps it will. In either case what is important is the listening that takes place, the respect and affirmation that it implies, and the dialogue that will inevitably follow.

'They Tie Up Heavy Burdens' Mt 23:4

Jesus was constantly critical of the scribes and Pharisees, and the way they practised their religion. They clearly got right under his skin, and his tirades against them show us a side of Jesus that we don't see anywhere else in the Gospel. He refers to them as 'hypocrites', 'blind guides', 'blind fools', 'snakes', and 'brood of vipers', language that seems totally out of character with Jesus' personality. Even the Roman soldiers, and Pontius Pilate himself, are treated with more courtesy and deference.

What was it about the religious leaders of the day that made Jesus so angry? Certainly their hypocrisy was at the heart of it, but it was really the fact that their hypocrisy resulted in burdens being placed on the people, burdens that they were not prepared to bear themselves.

The scribes and Pharisees were responsible for the way the Jewish religious rules and guidelines were interpreted and applied, and they were very strict in the way they carried out this role. They insisted that the people complied rigidly with every aspect of the law, including the payment of the temple tax. They oversaw numerous customs and traditions, rites and ceremonies, many of which were expensive and time consuming. They had no problem loading these burdens on people's shoulders, and, as Jesus points out, they were 'unwilling to lift a finger to move them'. To make matters worse, they were far less demanding on themselves, seeking the comforts of life, and quite prepared to neglect the law when it suited them.

We clergy have to constantly reflect on Jesus words to the religious leaders of his time. The same factors that allowed the scribes and Pharisees to be hard on the people, and easy on themselves, are still present in religious institutions today, and certainly in the Church. The clergy are the 'professionals' in the Catholic community. We get paid for what we do. We are not volunteers, and sometimes we can forget how difficult it is to volunteer one's time and energy to the Church, over and above the work and family commitments that most people have, and the clergy do not have. In other words, we can place expectations on the laity that we ourselves do not have to meet.

I have often heard priests say, when they are running late for Mass, 'Well, they can't start without me'. It is a throwaway line, intending to be humorous, but it can also hide an attitude of self-importance. It's particularly relevant in the case of priests and bishops who constantly start Mass late, being prepared to inconvenience others rather than make the effort to be on time.

Another way the clergy can burden parishioners is by preaching long homilies. 'If you cannot say it in ten minutes, you can't say it', is an expression with a lot of truth in it. I am not advocating that a homily could never go more than ten minutes, but most never should.

The majority of clergy seem to think that they are excellent preachers, and that people are happy to hear them speak. Some priests regularly preach for twenty minutes or more, and do not realise that most of the congregation have tuned out after ten minutes. I have a theory that in most cases, the longer the homily, the less preparation the priest has put into it, otherwise, while preparing the homily, he would become aware that he is starting to repeat himself, or starting to ramble. I remember one of the teachers in the seminary one day saying to us, 'If you ever preach without preparing your homily, tell it in confession, because it's a sin'.

Another way that clergy can put burdens on parishioners is by expecting them to undergo long and demanding programs before receiving the sacraments. The RCIA (Rite of Christian Initiation of Adults) program is a case in point. Certainly, people becoming Catholic need to learn about the Catholic faith, but not everyone is suited to the RCIA program, with its long and demanding time frame of six months or more. Some people require a program that is more individually suited and more flexible, and perhaps less time consuming, particularly those who already have a basic knowledge of the Christian faith and have clearly made their decision to join the Church.

I am not saying that the RCIA program does not have its place. I am saying that we have to be careful that we are not fitting people to a program, rather than fitting a program to people.

'I Was Sent Only to the Lost Sheep of the House of Israel' Mt 15:24

The doctrine of the Incarnation states that Jesus is both fully human and fully divine. It is one of the great mysteries of our faith. As a child growing up I had little problem accepting Jesus' divinity. We learnt the stories about his miraculous birth, about the various miracles that he worked, about how he knew things that no one else knew, how he could read people's minds. In fact, I probably had an image of Jesus as a kind of superman, wearing his humanity like an overcoat.

It was only in later years that I was challenged by the doctrine that Jesus was fully human, that he got frustrated and angry, that he felt pain and fear and sadness, that he didn't always know what would happen next.

The story of Jesus' encounter with the Canaanite woman shows a very human side of Jesus' character. It shows him wrestling with a dilemma that has consequences for his whole mission in life.

The Canaanite woman approaches Jesus and tells him that her daughter is sick, hoping that Jesus might be able to help her. But Jesus replies, 'I was sent only to the lost sheep of the house of Israel'. In other words, he felt that his mission was to his own Jewish people, and that he should not deviate from this path. But the woman persists. She comes and kneels before him saying, 'Lord, help me'. Even at this point Jesus is reluctant to do anything, but as the conversation continues he finally comes around, and grants her request.

Sometimes we just have to make exceptions, as Jesus does on this occasion. It is not an easy thing to do, as it implies that there is something not quite right with our original stance, whether that be an opinion, a formal position, or a law. Jesus clearly saw his ministry as being directed towards his own Jewish people. Even after his death the early Church continued to see themselves as part of the Jewish religious community. But something made Jesus make an exception on this occasion. He knew in his heart that he could not refuse to help this woman. Her need overrode his theology.

Many clergy find it difficult to make exceptions, especially when it relates to Church guidelines and practices. One case, for example, where surely an exception can be made, relates to the question of who can receive Holy Communion at a nursing home Mass. I have been constantly amazed by priests who refuse to offer Holy Communion in nursing homes to residents who are not Catholic.

Nursing home Masses are very special experiences. They bring together people from diverse religious backgrounds, and, of course, many of them are elderly and frail. Some of those who are not Catholic do not wish to receive Communion, but still love being part of the celebration. Then there are others who have clearly been receiving Communion in their own Christian tradition, and wish to continue receiving Communion at the Catholic Mass. They share a common understanding of the Eucharist, even if it might not be exactly the same as the Catholic formulation. But how could you not offer them Holy Communion? How could you not make an exception in those cases, particularly as those people are not able to go to their own churches?

'Do You Know What I Have Done to You?' Jn 13:12

When Jesus got down on his knees at the Last Supper and washed the feet of his disciples, he was expressing a very powerful message about who he is, and about who his followers are, namely, foot-washers, people who are prepared to serve, and to serve unconditionally.

The disciples didn't quite get the message. Peter, in particular, thought that Jesus should not have to perform such a humble act of servitude. But Jesus reminds him that a willingness to serve is the one thing, perhaps the most basic thing, that they share in common, and without it they are like strangers to each other.

The foot-washing ceremony has always had a special place in the Holy Thursday liturgy, and so it should. Even though it came out of a different era and a different culture, it still reminds us in a very profound way that ultimately Christian faith is about service, and service in a practical way, otherwise, like Peter, Christians will have nothing in common with Jesus.

The foot-washing ceremony has particular relevance for the priest. It is sometimes said that there are only two types of priests, those who get ordained to serve, and those who get ordained to be served. Perhaps, in reality, it is a little more nuanced than that, but the fact remains that we priests have to continually remind ourselves that we are there to serve, and not to be served, because in reality many people say to us what Peter said to Jesus, 'We should be washing your feet, not you washing ours'.

The foot-washing ceremony at the Mass of the Lord's Supper has taken different forms over the years. For a long time, the priest used to only wash the feet of twelve men. The argument was that Jesus washed the feet of twelve men, and so we should do the same if we are going to be faithful to the tradition.

Gradually women and children also began having their feet washed. In some cases the priest too, instead of being the only foot-washer, started to have his own feet washed as well. Pope Francis caused a lot of controversy when he celebrated Mass on his first Holy Thursday as Pope, and chose to wash the feet of both men and women, not all of whom were Catholic. In doing so he made an important statement, that the foot-washing ceremony is more than just role-playing. It is not about the number of people getting their feet washed, or their gender, or even their religion. It is about the meaning of the ceremony, and applying that meaning, that message of service, in a modern setting.

I have already noted how difficult it is for the hierarchy, and indeed for the clergy generally, to embrace change, and to do things in a way they have not traditionally been done in the past. It's always much easier to stay with what we are familiar with. The fact that Pope Francis was prepared to change the Holy Thursday foot-washing ritual in such a radical way says not only a lot about the place of service in the Christian life, but also about how we must be prepared to move away from traditional ways of doing things, if they are no longer relevant to our modern society, and to the contemporary Church.

Clergy or Laity? Where Does Jesus Fit In?

Before concluding this section, there is one more question that needs to be addressed, and it relates to Jesus' role and position within his own Jewish community. 'Was Jesus a member of the clergy, or was he a lay person?' In one sense it is a bit of a trick question. Theologically we refer to Jesus as the High Priest, the one from whom all Christian priesthood takes its meaning. But that comes out of a later reflection on Jesus' life, and death. Obviously, there was no Christian priesthood in Jesus' day.

It is also clear that Jesus was not part of the Jewish priestly class. He did not do anything that would suggest he took on a priestly role among the Jewish religious leaders. Indeed, his strong and continual criticism of their attitudes and practices suggests that he could never have performed priestly duties in that religious culture.

So, we ask the question again, 'Was Jesus a cleric or a lay person?' Well, perhaps in Jesus time there could have been something in the middle. Jesus was certainly a religious preacher of some note. People came to listen to him in great numbers, travelling long distances to hear his words. He read the Scriptures in the temple, and preached there. People called him Rabbi, and Teacher. He had a certain religious standing, even among the scribes and Pharisees. While they did not agree with what he said and did, they recognised his influential position among the people, and were always trying to bring him down. Perhaps we could say that Jesus had an informal priestly ministry, but in any strict sense, he was a lay person.

People will have different positions on this question, depending on how they see priestly ministry in general, and how they interpret Jesus' own ministry in particular. To me the interesting aspect is that we are still not sure. And this is precisely because Jesus showed no disconnection with the people he ministered to. There was no other group he belonged to, no club, no insiders, no priestly class. Even the twelve disciples, with whom he spent so much time, received no special favours. Jesus is as quick to challenge them as he is to challenge the scribes and Pharisees. In other words, he is the perfect expression of true ministry, so inclusive that it is impossible to categorise, so all-embracing that it is impossible to stereotype. On the one hand, Jesus' ministry is the model for all lay ministry, and on the other hand, the model for all priestly ministry.

The Scriptures tell us that at the moment Jesus died on Calvary, the veil of the temple was torn in two, from top to bottom (Mt 27:51). It is quite a curious incident to be placed immediately after Jesus' death. There are various interpretations of the event, but I like to think that it says something about Jesus' relationship with his people.

The temple veil was a huge thick curtain that could have been as long as twenty metres, stretching up to the ceiling of the temple. It separated the Holy of Holies, the area revered as God's dwelling place, from the rest of the temple, where people gathered for ceremonies and prayer. The Holy of Holies was off limits for the laity. Only the priests were able to pass beyond the veil.

When Jesus took his last breath, and the temple veil was torn in two, there is a beautiful symbolism reminding us that the Holy of Holies is no longer restricted territory, that there are no longer any barriers between God and ourselves, no veils of any sort, nothing, as Saint Paul puts it, that 'will be able to separate us from the love of God in Christ Jesus Our Lord' (Rom 8:39).

But there is a secondary symbolism in the tearing of the temple veil at the time of Jesus' death. It also reminds us that there is no longer a barrier between the clergy and the laity. There is no longer a holy place where the priests can go, and the laity cannot go. The holy place where God dwells is for all.

Conclusion to Part 4

In this section I have looked, at least briefly, at Jesus life and his ministry. We have seen him respond to a variety of people in different situations, and have gained an insight into his personality, his faith, and his sense of solidarity with those around him. He clearly feels a strong connection to people, no matter what their background or status in life. There is certainly no attitude of aloofness or superiority in his manner. He is humble and respectful to all. He does not expect to be treated with special deference, or to receive any special privileges. In other words, there is not the slightest element of clericalism in Jesus, or any sort of club mentality.

Part 5
Pope Francis—A Sign of Hope

It is very unusual for a bishop to publicly criticise the clergy. It is even more unusual for the Pope to do it. It is true that both Pope Benedict and Pope John Paul II made statements warning about the dangers of a clerical culture in the Church, but those statements were limited in their force and impact. Criticism of clericalism within the hierarchy, or indeed criticism of the clergy in any way, has never been high on the papal agenda.

But that all changed on 13 March 2013, when Jorge Mario Bergoglio was elected Pope, taking the name Francis. In fact, a lot changed in the Church on that day. Pope Francis brought a new freshness to the papacy that we hadn't seen for many years. His warm smile and personable manner endeared not only those from the Catholic community to him, but people of all faiths, and none. His informal style and off the cuff remarks made him look 'normal', and vulnerable. But it's his comments on clericalism that have gained most attention, heartening many, while at the same time drawing criticism from more conservative quarters.

It is not the first time that members of the clergy have pointed out the dangers of clericalism in the Church. Indeed, in recent years the criticism seems to be getting stronger and more widespread. But when the pope leads the charge, then it is different. Pope Francis is the top cleric, and what he says about the clerical culture in the Church sets the tone for other bishops and priests, indeed for the Church generally.

So, what has Pope Francis said?

The Evil of Clericalism

On 13 December 2016, the Vatican newspaper, *L'Osservatore Romano* records Pope Francis saying that 'The spirit of clericalism is an evil that is present in the Church today'. 'Clerics feel they are superior, they are far from the people.'[1]

This notion of superiority is at the heart of clericalism, and certainly fundamental to Pope Francis' understanding of the phenomenon. It is not a superiority born of arrogance. It is a superiority that comes out of a Church structure and culture that continually reinforces the idea that the priest is special, in a way that other people are not special, that the priest is sacred, in a way that other people are not sacred, that the priest is another Christ, in a way that other people are not other Christs. It is not hard to see how an attitude of superiority can develop when these forces are constantly at work.

On 19 March 2016, in a letter to Cardinal Marc Quellet, President of the Pontifical Commission of Latin America, Pope Francis notes that clericalism 'forgets that the visibility and the sacramentality of the Church belong to all the people of God and not just to an illuminated and elected few'.[2] The 'illuminated and elected few', of course, are the 'superior' ones.

That word 'illuminated' is very important. Some of the clergy, because of the amount of studies they have done, and the degrees they have attained, along with the fact that they have been given the sacrament of Holy Orders, feel they have greater insights into faith, and into an understanding of God, than the laity. There can be a sense that God has instilled some special knowledge into them.

I am not suggesting, of course, that study in Church matters is not important. Indeed, for Church leaders it is essential to have a good grounding in theology, philosophy, scripture, and other related subjects. The problem arises when the attainment of knowledge beguiles the priest into thinking that he is above the rest of the community in some way, or as Pope Francis puts it, they become 'intellectuals of religion', who are 'seduced by clericalism'.[3]

---

1. Pope Francis' homily from Mass at the Casa Santa Marta, 13 December, 2016, Vatican Radio, the Voice of the Pope and the Church in Dialogue with the World.
2. Letter of His Holiness Pope Francis to Cardinal Marc Quellet, President of the Pontifical Commission of Latin America, Vatican City, 19 March, 2016.
3. Pope Francis' homily from Mass at the Casa Santa Marta.

Pope Francis himself is a great example of a member of the clergy who can minister and lead without displaying any sense of superiority. He does not pretend to have all the answers, which is particularly refreshing, because, as Pope, many people expect him to have all the answers. While not wishing to make too much of the comment, his response, 'Who am I to judge?' to a question about homosexuality, certainly shows a man who is open to listening and learning.

Pope Francis is truly a sign of hope in the struggle to confront the clergy club mentality, while at the same time presenting a clergy mentality himself that is inclusive and welcoming.

Clericalism and the Laity

Pope Francis' strident criticism of clericalism has surprised and upset quite a few people in the Church, particularly among the clergy themselves. Has he gone too far? What is it that is pushing him to say this?

Well, certainly we can say that Pope Francis sees clericalism as a real danger to the Church, and something that he wants to see stamped out as soon as possible. 'One of the gravest dangers', he says, 'stronger in the Church today, is clericalism'.[4]

The language he uses about clericalism is indeed very strident and passionate. 'The evil of clericalism', he says, 'is a very ugly thing'.[5] The words 'evil' and 'ugly' are strong words. Pope Francis clearly gets angry when he sees any form of clericalism around him. And his anger comes from a belief that clericalism hurts the laity, and attempts to diminish their standing in the community. In fact, when talking about the spirit of clericalism, Pope Francis claims that 'the victim of this spirit is the people, who feel discarded and abused'.[6] In another instance, he says that clericalism 'not only nullifies the character of Christians, but also tends to diminish and undervalue the baptismal grace that the Holy Spirit has placed in the heart of our people'.[7] And continuing the theme, the pope says, 'It does us good to remember that the Church is not an elite of priests, of consecrated men, of bishops, but that everyone forms the faithful Holy People of God'.[8]

---

4. Pope Francis' address to the Order of Clerics Regular of Somasca, 30 March, 2017, Vatican Apostolic Palace.
5. Pope Francis' homily from Mass at the Casa Santa Marta.
6. Pope Francis' homily from Mass at the Casa Santa Marta.
7. Letter of His Holiness Pope Francis to Cardinal Marc Quellet.
8. Letter of His Holiness Pope Francis to Cardinal Marc Quellet.

In one way or another, all these statements are saying the same thing, that the laity have an essential role to play in the Church, and that clericalism, or more correctly, clergy with an attitude of clericalism, seek to take that role away from them.

Control

Pope Francis also points out that at the heart of clericalism is a desire to control. He is very strong on the idea that the laity have been 'anointed' to exercise their rightful ministry in the Church, and says that clericalism 'seeks to control, and put a break on this anointment by God of the faithful'.[9] In reference to the laity working in public life, he says that 'It is not the job of the pastor to tell the lay people what they must do and say'.[10] 'It's illogical', Pope Francis says, 'and even impossible for us as pastors to believe that we have the monopoly on solutions for the numerous challenges thrown up by contemporary life'.[11]

The temptation for the clergy to control the laity is certainly strong, and ever present. The clergy have absolute power at all levels in the Church, and while the laity can offer their opinion, it is always only an opinion or suggestion. For the clergy to relinquish control, they have to actually invite the laity into the decision-making process, and then be prepared to work together with the laity in a genuinely collegial way. It is not impossible, but it has never been part of the clergy culture.

Pope Francis is certainly doing his part to try and change that culture. 'Work with the laity', he told a group of priests in Rome for their General Chapter. 'Let them go ahead.'[12]

The Prophetic Flame

Pope Francis also makes the point that clericalism attempts to silence the prophetic voice of the Church. 'Clericalism, far from inspiring various contributions and proposals', he says, 'gradually extinguishes the prophetic flame of which the entire Church is called to bear witness in the heart of her peoples'.[13]

---

9. Letter of His Holiness Pope Francis to Cardinal Marc Quellet.
10. Letter of His Holiness Pope Francis to Cardinal Marc Quellet.
11. Letter of His Holiness Pope Francis to Cardinal Marc Quellet.
12. Pope Francis' address to the Order of Clerics Regular of Somasca.
13. Letter of His Holiness Pope Francis to Cardinal Marc Quellet.

I personally believe that this is one of the most dangerous consequences of clericalism. The Church that Jesus founded is called to be a prophetic Church, a Church inspired by the Spirit, a Church that is not afraid to speak out, and to risk. Clericalism, on the other hand, fosters an attitude of safety and security, an unwillingness to 'put out into the deep water' (Lk 5:4). It turns the Church into a functionary Church, holding the fort, doing what has to be done, hesitant to leave familiar shores.

One of the effects of the clerical mindset is that the Church stops being a leader in the community, and instead it becomes a follower. Its leaders no longer inspire, because they have allowed themselves to be caught up in rituals and rules, rather than proclaiming the radical message of the Gospel. They cannot move forward, even in simple, practical ways, so great is the inertia and passivity that clericalism engenders.

An example of the way clericalism 'extinguishes the prophetic flame' is seen in the manner in which the hierarchy responds to those members of the clergy who dare to break ranks and speak out about what they believe to be wrong in the Church. In Australia, there have been a number of bishops who have spoken out against clericalism in one form or another, but they have never been publicly supported by their colleagues. It's no wonder that many clergy are very wary about saying anything that could be interpreted as a criticism of the Church.

Ultimately clericalism is incompatible with the prophetic voice of the Spirit and the visionary nature of the Gospel. Pope Francis is right. If clericalism flourishes, the flame will be extinguished.

'It Takes Two to Tango'

Pope Francis makes an interesting comment when he says that 'Clericalism is a negative attitude, and it requires complicity'.[14] He goes on to say that it is 'something done by two parties, just as it takes two to tango, that is, the priest wants to clericalize the layman, the laywoman, the man or woman religious, and the lay person asks to be clericalized, because it is easier that way. And this is odd'.

---

14. Address of His Holiness Pope Francis to the International Union of Superiors General, Rome, 12 May 2016.

In the same talk he says, 'In Latin America clericalism is very strong and pronounced. Lay people do not know what to do, if they do not ask the priest'.[15]

Pope Francis is making the point that clericalism has not only become part of the clergy culture, but is now also part of the lay culture, in the sense that the laity have grown so used to always deferring to the priest that they have forgotten how to act otherwise, or see no point in getting involved. Certainly, in some parishes, parishioners feel there is not much point going on parish councils or liturgy committees or finance committees, because they feel the parish priest will do what he wants to do anyway. They are happy just to help out where they can, as, in the words of Pope Francis, 'it is easier that way'.

There is also a hesitancy among many parishioners to challenge the priest, even when they feel something should be said. It is a big thing for a committed Catholic to openly question the parish priest, or decisions that he has made. It has never been part of Catholic culture and it certainly is easier to remain silent.

Perhaps, too, this hesitancy to get involved relates to the fact that in some cases the laity are quite happy with a clerical culture, and, as Pope Francis puts it, actually ask to be clericalised. They prefer to see the priest doing everything, and making all the decisions himself, while they play a more traditional, passive role in the parish. Once again it is certainly 'easier that way'.

Pope Francis' statement that clericalism 'requires complicity' between the clergy and the laity is a challenge to both parties to do something about it. It is not just a problem for the clergy to deal with. The laity have a role in helping to expose clericalism for what it is, and helping the clergy to see it for what it is. Indeed, this role of the laity is part of the Church's prophetic voice, ensuring that the flame is never extinguished.

Jesus and Clericalism

In his homily on 13 December 2016, at Casa Santa Marta in Rome, Pope Francis speaks about the priestly culture in Jesus' day. Like Jesus himself 2000 years ago, the Pope is highly critical of the attitude the

---

15. Address of His Holiness Pope Francis to the International Union of Superiors General, Rome, 12 May 2016.

chief priests and the elders displayed towards the Jewish people. 'With the law they themselves had made", he says, "they cancelled the law the Lord had made, they lacked the memory that connects the current moment with Revelation.' They showed 'arrogance and tyranny towards the people'.[16]

And then Pope Francis speaks about Jesus, and the decision he had to make between the chief priests and the elders on the one hand, or the poor and the marginalised on the other. In a most insightful passage he says, 'the Father has always sought to be close to us: He sent his Son. We are waiting in joyful expectation, exulting. But the Son didn't join in the game of these people: The Son went with the sick, the poor, the discarded, the publicans, the sinners'.[17]

The Son did not join in the game! What a powerful way of expressing Jesus' 'No' to clericalism.

Fifteen Sicknesses of the Roman Curia

On 22 December 2014 Pope Francis addressed members of the Roman curia, comprising cardinals, bishops and priests, all of whom are involved in the management of the central administration of the Church. He tells them that the curia, like every human body, 'is also exposed to disease, malfunction, infirmity'.[18] He then goes on to list fifteen of these 'curial diseases', which he believes occur most frequently.

As Pope Francis points out, these 'diseases' represent a danger for all Christians and all communities, but his words are specifically addressed to the clergy who work in the curia. Clearly, therefore, the Pope recognises that these problems have particular relevance to bishops and priests.

I am not going to name all the issues that Pope Francis addresses, although each of them, in one way or another, says something about clericalism. I will just mention four, that in a particular way encourage and reinforce a clergy club mentality. I won't add any commentary to the Pope's words. They speak for themselves, and their connection to the club mentality is obvious.

---

16. Pope Francis' homily at the Mass at the Casa Santa Marta.
17. Pope Francis' homily at the Mass at the Casa Santa Marta.
18. Address of His Holiness Pope Francis, 'The Roman Curia and the Body of Christ', 22 December 2014, Rome.

The first is what Pope Francis calls 'the disease of thinking we are "immortal", 'immune' or downright "indispensable"'. 'It is a disease', he says, 'of those who turn into lords and masters, and think of themselves as above others and not at their service'. It derives from 'a superiority complex', and 'the pathology of power'.

Then there is 'the disease of mental and spiritual "petrification"'. 'It is found in those who have a heart of stone'. It is found in 'those who lose the human sensitivity that enables us to weep with those who weep and to rejoice with those who rejoice'. It is the disease of 'those who lose the "sentiments of Jesus"'.

Another one is 'the disease of excessive planning and functionalism'. 'Things need to be prepared well', says Pope Francis, 'but without ever falling into the temptation of trying to contain and direct the freedom of the Holy Spirit'. We contract this disease because 'it is always more easy and comfortable to settle in our own sedentary and unchanging ways'.

Finally, there is what Pope Francis calls 'the disease of a lugubrious face'. Here he is referring to 'those glum and dour persons who think that to be serious we have to put on a face of melancholy and severity, and treat others—especially those we consider our inferiors—with rigour, brusqueness and arrogance'. The Pope then adds, 'in fact, a show of severity and sterile pessimism are frequently symptoms of fear and insecurity'.

Personal Conversion

Pope Francis has clearly been thinking deeply about clericalism in the Church, about reform of the clergy, and about how that reform might take place. He has set up numerous commissions to help bring about structural change in the Church, and particularly in the Vatican itself. But as he notes in his 'Twelve Guiding Principles for the Reform of the Curia', without personal conversion "all structural change would prove useless". 'The true soul of the reform', he says, 'are the men and women who are part of it and make it possible'.[19]

In other words, eradicating clericalism from the Church will never happen unless the clergy themselves make a decision that it must be done. As with all problems, nothing can be achieved until there is an acceptance that the problem exists.

---

19. Address by Pope Francis to members of the Roman Curia, 22 December, 2016, Vatican City.

A Pope Who Smiles

One of the most engaging qualities of Pope Francis is his sense of joy. He smiles a lot. He seems to be very comfortable in his own skin. He clearly enjoys his work, and his ministry. And most importantly, the way he proclaims the Gospel message expresses that same sense of joy and celebration.

It is always a constant challenge for us as clergy to make sure that we proclaim the message of Jesus as 'good news', not 'bad news', just as Jesus did himself. It is not something that we always do well, and certainly clericalism does not help in this regard. If our attitude is too focussed on rules and regulations, on judgment and penance, then our proclamation of the Gospel will come across as pessimistic and uninviting, rather than joyful and welcoming. And a Gospel that is preached without joy is not the Gospel of Jesus.

Pope Francis reminds everyone in the Church that being a Christian, and a Catholic, should be an uplifting experience. He particularly challenges the clergy not to preach a message of doom and gloom, but one of hope and optimism.

'Do Not Feel Different from Your Peers'

In December 2016, Pope Francis gave a talk to a group of Italian seminarians from the Puglia region. He spoke specifically about the danger of the clergy becoming disconnected from the laity. 'Do not feel different from your peers', he told them. 'If tomorrow you will be priests who live in the midst of the holy people of God, begin today to be young people who know how to be with everyone, who can learn something from every person you meet, with humility and intelligence.'[20]

In these words, Pope Francis highlights two fundamental attitudes that are needed to change the clergy club mentality. Firstly, he identifies a sense of solidarity and oneness with the laity, expressed in the phrase 'know how to be with everyone', and secondly, a genuine sense of humility in relation to the laity, expressed in the phrase 'learn something from every person you meet'. This is the challenge for every member of the clergy, to put these two qualities into practice, and if that can be done, then clericalism will eventually become a thing of the past.

---

20. Address of His Holiness Pope Francis to the Community of the Pontifical Regional Seminary of Apulia Pio XI, 10 December, 2016, Rome.

The Francis Effect

The popularity of Pope Francis is quite extraordinary. People everywhere are responding to his warmth, his simplicity, his humility and his serenity. He has brought a new sense of optimism to the Church. This effect that Pope Francis has had on the Church, and beyond, has become known as 'The Francis Effect'.

But why does Pope Francis evoke such a response? What he is saying is certainly not new. It has all been said before. Jesus said it 2000 years ago. But that is exactly the point. Pope Francis is saying exactly what Jesus said. In fact, so much of what he says comes straight from the Gospel. His words about clericalism in particular, echo the words that Jesus addressed to the priests of his day. So, it is not so much a "Francis effect" that we are talking about here, but rather a 'Jesus effect', personified in a Pope who understands the real message of the Gospel.

Normalising the Papacy

Pope Francis received enormous publicity from the first moment he became Pope, and sometimes for rather curious reasons. One of the very first stories that gained international headlines was how he personally paid a hotel bill, and then took a ride in a taxi, rather than in a limousine. People found it quite extraordinary that a Pope would do such ordinary things.

In a way Pope Francis has 'normalised' the papacy. I do not use that word in any off-handed or disparaging way. I mean that Pope Francis has taken some of the pomp and ceremony, and perhaps some of the mystique, out of the papacy. He fulfils the role with great dignity and respect, but in so many ways he is saying that he personally is no better than anyone else, just trying to do the best he can with what he has to offer.

In a similar way, I feel there is a need to 'normalise' the priesthood. And once again I use the word very carefully. The priesthood is a wonderful vocation. It hardly needs to be said. But priests themselves are just normal people, trying to do the best they can with what they have to offer. Unless the clergy can accept their own 'normality', as Pope Francis clearly can, they will never be able to truly connect with the laity.

Part 6
A Way Forward

And, so, where to from here?

In the preceding pages I spoke about what the clergy club mentality is, where it comes from, how it expresses itself, and how it contrasts with the example Jesus set for us in his own life and ministry. I then reflected on some of the numerous statements that Pope Francis has made on clericalism in the Church today. Now it is time to look forward, to see if we can put some things in place that will make it possible for the clergy club mentality to be transformed into something more positive, more inclusive, and more life-giving.

Change in the Church

Some people say that it is impossible for the Church to change, as long as it remains in its present form. The argument is that the Church's culture is too entrenched, and the structures themselves are too strong and too rigid to allow new attitudes and new perspectives to flourish. All institutions, of course, are suspicious of change, and favour those policies, and indeed those people, who will maintain the status quo. The Church, in particular, finds it very difficult to change because of its sheer size and its long history and tradition. Added to this is the notion that much of the Church's teaching is held to be revealed by God, and so is seen as divine and unchangeable.

Another reason that change is very slow in the Church is because the structure is top down. In most other institutions, and in society generally, change tends to come from the bottom up. More and more these days, in institutions right across the board, a great deal of time and money is spent on finding out how the people in the organisation think and feel. Their opinions are sought, and their views taken seriously.

In the Church however, the views of the laity are not sought in the same way, or given the same level of importance. In a top down structure like the Church, decisions can only be made from above. As in the case of the Third Rite of Reconciliation, it is possible for the vast majority of Church members to want a particular practice or policy put in place, but if the bishops do not want it, it won't happen.

It is sometimes argued that change will not come about in the Church without a third Vatican Council. In a top down structure like the Church it is clearly difficult for the person at the top, the pope, to change anything of real importance. He would be always known as the pope who changed the Church's position on that particular teaching or practice. Thus, in reality, change is only likely to happen when the bishops come together and share the decision-making responsibility in a communal way. Pope John XXIII, for example, would never have brought in the changes that we saw in the Church in the 1960s if it had been left to himself. But once he brought together the bishops of the world to a council, a new dynamic was in place, responsibility for decision-making was shared, and change could, and did, take place.

A Reason for Optimism

My words above paint a rather pessimistic picture of the Church's ability to change, particularly in regard to clericalism. But I remain hopeful. I can see a number of elements in the Church today that are working towards breaking down the club mentality.

The first one is simply that there is a feeling of change in the air. The Church today is a very different Church to that of even twenty years ago. Sadly, one of the main reasons for that shift is the child sexual abuse crisis, and, at least here in Australia, the Royal Commission that followed. These shocking crimes committed by Catholic clergy, and the lack of proper responses by many Church authorities, have caused so much suffering to the victims and their families, but they have also forced the hierarchy to do some serious soul-searching. Things cannot go on as they have in the past. Bishops realise that as a group they have not always made good decisions. In fact, at times they have made terrible decisions. They acknowledge that they must listen more carefully, and be more open to change, particularly change in the clerical culture. If this attitude endures into the future, then there is real hope for a closer relationship between the laity and the clergy.

For the second reason why I feel change in the clergy club mentality is possible, I return to Pope Francis. I have already spoken about Pope Francis, and the new sense of hope and freshness he has brought to the Church. I have spoken, too, about the comments and criticisms he has made about clericalism in the clergy ranks. But there is another consequence of Pope Francis style and attitude that is significant, and that is the fact that he has legitimised a new perspective on the Church that is more Gospel centred and certainly less clerical. He has legitimised the pushing of boundaries, as he himself has done on numerous occasions. He has legitimised asking questions about whether, as a Church, the things we have done in the past can be done in new and better ways in the future.

Any priest who has stood up at a clergy conference in the past, and challenged some of the attitudes or policies of the Church, knows that something now has changed. Under the papacy of John Paul II, and then under Benedict, it was difficult for new ideas to get any traction at all, particularly if those ideas were about a greater role for the laity in the Church. Today, however, the mood is different. When suggestions are made that might help to make the local Church more inclusive, more people-orientated, less clerical, less rigid, those views resonate with the views of Pope Francis, and are now taken more seriously.

Another reason for optimism, with regard to change in the Church, is that there is so much goodwill among all members of the Church community. There is certainly an enormous amount of goodwill among the priests and bishops, and while the clergy may hold a range of different views, they all want the best for the Church, as they see it. Yes, there are those on the conservative side who would like to see parish Masses once again celebrated in Latin, and those on the progressive side who would like to see more variety and flexibility in the Sunday liturgy, but there can be no doubting the fact that every member of the clergy wants both the Church and the priesthood to flourish, and be the best Church, and the best priesthood, it can be. I am hopeful that this goodwill among the clergy will bring about genuine dialogue, and an openness to change, and that can only result in a better relationship between the laity and the clergy.

Finally, I would like to make the point that what I am talking about here is not a change in Church teaching or doctrine, but a change in attitude, primarily a change in the mentality of the clergy, but also a change in the mentality of the laity. It is not about changing the

Church's position on long held views. It is not about getting involved in deep theological arguments about whether a particular policy is in keeping with the Church's tradition. It is simply a discussion that involves looking at the laity/clergy relationship from a different perspective, and as such, it can be done without shaking the foundations of the Church's structures.

Vision and Practice

It cannot be denied that there are many people in the Catholic community who would love to see a Church that is more inclusive of the laity, more open to change, more prepared to engage in the modern world, and less caught up in religious trappings. Those of us old enough to remember the Second Vatican Council are particularly passionate about what the Church could be. At the time of the Council we saw a Church that for the first time in many centuries was showing signs of real change. We saw a Church that was beginning to look beyond itself, and see how it related to the rest of the world. We saw a Church starting to recognise that the role of the laity was every bit as important as the role of the clergy. And today we see a Pope who embodies the spirit of Vatican II, and that inspires a lot of hope.

But hope doesn't bring about change. Hope does not turn a vision into reality. Hope does not transform attitudes. The only way these things can happen is through action.

The 1,000 Kilometre Walk

There is a saying that a journey of 1,000 kilometres starts with a first step. That first modest step seems quite insignificant, but it represents the beginning of something momentous. Clericalism in the Church will not be eradicated unless there is a first step, a first practical step on the way to bringing about something momentous.

With this in mind I would like to propose a first step, or perhaps I should say a series of first steps, on the way to changing the clergy club mentality. It takes the form of eight practical suggestions that I believe, if implemented, will transform the clergy club mentality into something far more open and inclusive, and thus help to break down the disconnection between clergy and laity.

None of the proposals is earth-shattering, and they are certainly not new. They don't challenge any theological principles, and they are all easy to implement. But if they could be put into practice, it would represent a strong willingness on the part of the hierarchy to respond to the challenge that Pope Francis has put before us all, to eradicate the scourge of clericalism from the Church.

As I have already said, the proposals are modest. Many of them could take place with very few people even noticing. But in another sense the changes are not at all insignificant. In fact, they are extremely significant, because they are helping to shape a culture and an attitude. They have the potential to bring about real, positive and long-lasting benefits, not only for the clergy, but also for the laity.

Each of the suggestions relates to an issue I have mentioned earlier, and which I feel contributes to the club mentality of the clergy. Of course, there are many factors, certainly more than eight, that help to create a culture of clericalism, but at least in these eight specific areas I would like to propose some practical steps that I believe would really work in changing attitudes, and thus contribute towards overcoming the problem.

Proposal Number 1

There is no doubt that the Second Vatican Council challenged the laity to move from a passive, to a far more active participation in the life of the Church. The most obvious sign of this involvement of the laity was the growth in so many lay ministries in the parish. But the recognition of the role of the laity in the Church was not just about lay people doing more things, exercising more ministries. They were also encouraged to make a contribution to the decision-making process in the Church, to be involved in the Church's vision and direction, through such bodies as pastoral councils, social justice groups, liturgy committees, finance committees and others.

In the Decree on the Apostolate of the Laity,[1] Pope Paul VI reflects on St Paul's image of the Church as 'the Body of Christ' (1 Cor. 12:27). He states that 'no part of the structure of a living body is merely passive but has a share in the functions as well as life of the body'.[2] He

---

1. Decree on the Apostolate of the Laity, *Apostolocam Actuositatem* promulgated by His Holiness Pope Paul VI, 18 November, 1965.
2. Decree on the Apostolate of the Laity, *Apostolocam.*

then goes on to say that 'the member who fails to make his proper contribution to the development of the Church must be said to be useful neither to the Church nor to himself'.[3]

But I ask the question, how do the laity 'make their proper contribution to the development of the Church?' And indeed, why do so many members of the laity feel that they are 'useful neither to the Church nor to themselves?' The laity can only make their proper contribution to the Church when the hierarchy recognise and encourage that contribution.

While at the parish level there are often opportunities to contribute to the life of the Church, at the diocesan level it is very difficult for a layperson to have any input whatsoever. The committees and commissions where major issues are discussed and decisions made, are primarily, if not totally, constituted by the clergy. The bishops' conferences, the meetings of the council of priests, the clergy conferences, the deanery meetings, are all clergy gatherings. These are the meetings where the big topics are discussed, where the vision for the diocese is clarified, and where the agendas are set. And the laity have virtually no input into any of it. Lay people may be invited at times to give a presentation, but they are not part of the ongoing conversation.

Even when a bishop comes to visit a parish there is usually little opportunity for him to have any real dialogue with the community. Most of the time he is there for a Confirmation ceremony, or perhaps to open a new building, and, to be fair, the time is very tight. He celebrates the Mass, talks to a few people after Mass, and needs to move on to his next appointment.

But dialogue between the bishop and the community is essential if the diocese is to flourish and reach its full potential. The community needs to listen to the bishop, and the bishop needs to listen to the community. The community needs to be able to ask the bishop questions, and the bishop needs to be able to ask the community questions. Otherwise all the bishop ever hears is feedback from other bishops and priests. He fails to hear the voice of the laity, and the contribution they have a right to make.

It is true that on rare occasions the bishops have organised gatherings with the Australian laity to hear what they have to say on Church matters. These gatherings are called Plenary Councils. There is one being organised for 2020. The previous one took place in 1937.

---

3. Decree on the Apostolate of the Laity, *Apostolocam.*

Hopefully something positive will come out of the upcoming Plenary Council, but these gatherings occur so infrequently they can have little effect in bringing about a change in clerical culture or clergy mentality. Something more consistent and ongoing is necessary.

So how can we set up a model where a coming together of the clergy and the laity can take place on a more regular basis? How can we set up a situation where both the bishops and the laity feel comfortable partaking in serious and ongoing conversation about Church matters?

It is not easy to find a solution. The sheer size of the numbers presents a practical difficulty. Time is also an issue. Everyone is busy, both the laity and the clergy. And no matter what proposition is put forward, some will feel it is not adequate, or appropriate.

Having said that, I would like to propose an idea that I think might work.

All dioceses have regular clergy conferences. In the Sydney Archdiocese, the clergy conferences are well attended and run smoothly and efficiently. It is a good format and we get through a lot of work. And there is no reason why this same format would not work just as well with a group comprising both clergy and laity, in equal numbers.[4] Surely an annual one day gathering could be organised without too much difficulty, where the laity and clergy come together and share ideas, each one learning from the other's perspective.

What tends to happen currently is that there are separate gatherings of the laity, where they discuss 'lay issues', and separate gatherings of the clergy, where they discuss 'clergy issues'. But this is not how the Church should work. In reality, there are no such things as 'lay issues' and 'clergy issues'. All issues relating to the Church are relevant to every member of the Church. This is why laity and clergy must come together as one to address these issues.

How the lay people are selected for these gatherings is a matter for the local diocese. Perhaps they could be nominated from a wide cross section of the diocese. Perhaps a panel, comprising both clergy and laity, could be set up with the purpose of deciding the make-up of the group. The agenda, too, would have to be agreed upon by both groups. All these issues can be sorted out.

---

4. I am very aware that equal numbers of clergy and laity present at a Church conference is not representative of their respective numbers in the Catholic community, with the laity making up the vast majority of Church membership. However, at this stage, it is probably the best that can be hoped for.

The important thing is that a group of clergy and laity, of manageable size, would be coming together to dialogue on important matters concerning the work of the Church. Just to see such a group in action would be inspirational. It would certainly be the first time that we had seen anything like it in the Sydney Archdiocese. Apart from anything else, it would be making a statement, a very powerful statement, about the importance of the relationship between the clergy and the laity.

And so, my first suggestion is: *that an annual conference be organised in the diocese, where both clergy and laity come together in equal numbers to discuss relevant issues relating to the Church.*

Proposal Number 2

Priests tend to see themselves as different to everyone else, especially in the area of employment. Priests do not talk about themselves as having a job, but rather having a vocation. They do not see themselves as doing work, but rather doing ministry. They do not receive an income, but rather a stipend. It is not hard to imagine that if priests see themselves as outside the normal work environment, then it's a short step to seeing themselves as outside the normal accountability environment.

Everyone who carries out paid work in society has to be accountable for the quality of the work they do. Whether you are a schoolteacher, a butcher, a company director or a pilot, you have to show that you are competent in carrying out your job, and that you are willing to keep developing your skills.

Priests and bishops have never been used to this type of accountability. It has always been assumed that the clergy are good men, and are doing their best. To ask a member of the clergy to do some sort of professional appraisal would, at least in the past, be almost seen as an insult, bringing the priest down to the level of everyone else, and implying that he may be able to do better in the exercise of his ministry.

But that attitude cannot continue any longer. Priests and bishops must be as accountable as anyone else in society. The parishioners deserve it. They have a right to have their religious leaders providing the best quality ministry possible. And the clergy, for their part, have a right to be challenged, so that they can be the best priests and bishops they can be.

In practice, this accountability would require some sort of appraisal process, which could take many forms. A number of priests in the diocese, including myself, have done such an appraisal, some of us more than once. It is challenging. Any time that you put yourself under the scrutiny of others, especially in such a formal way, in the work environment, you open yourself up to the possibility of having to face some home truths. But it is also extremely rewarding. Appraisals are essentially about affirming the strengths of the person being appraised, while at the same time looking for ways to improve areas of weakness.

Unfortunately, there is still a degree of reluctance among priests and bishops regarding appraisals. It has never been part of the clergy culture and so there is a certain anxiousness about what it may entail. There is also the issue that priests tend to see their priestly work and their personal lives as very closely connected, perhaps in some cases, even the same thing. Many therefore find it difficult to see how their ministry can be appraised without them being appraised as people. And nobody wants those sorts of personal judgements made about themselves.

The other issue regarding clergy appraisals centres on what happens to the appraisal after it is completed. Who gets to read the report? One would expect that the bishop would read the report and have a conversation with the priest about its contents. But some priests are concerned about this, understandably, as the priest's relationship with the bishop is a complex one. It includes not only a workplace dimension, but also a pastoral dimension.

But these issues aren't insurmountable. I am confident that once priests and bishops start undertaking appraisals they will have a far more positive perspective on the process, and see the real benefits that come out of it. They will certainly get a better idea of how the parishioners see, and value, their ministry, and that can only help to break down the club mentality.

And so, my second suggestion is: *that all priests and bishops in the diocese undergo a professional appraisal process at least once every three years.*

Proposal Number 3

The sign of peace at Mass has never sat comfortably with many parishioners, nor indeed with many of the clergy. Some people feel uneasy about greeting a person they may not know, or just feel that the whole gesture is a bit awkward or stilted. Others are more concerned about the hygiene side, shaking the hand of a stranger just before receiving Communion. Others, particularly among the clergy, feel that it can easily get out of hand and disturb the continuity of the Mass.

They are all valid points, and need to be taken seriously, but maybe that's just what making peace entails, feeling a bit uneasy and awkward, being prepared to accept the dangers that come with welcoming a stranger, and wondering if all this peace will get out of hand.

But whatever our particular perspective, the sign of peace at Mass is certainly a very powerful reminder that the worshipping community is fundamentally a community of peace, and it is that peace, Jesus' peace, that binds us together.

I find it hard to understand, then, why the Congregation for Divine Worship and the Discipline of the Sacrament, in the 2004 Instruction *Redemptionis Sacramentum*[5] forbids the priest or bishop who is celebrating Mass from leaving the sanctuary to give the sign of peace to parishioners in the body of the Church. Surely this just reinforces the view that there is a barrier, a disconnection between the laity and the clergy, rather than expressing the bond that exists between everyone in the community, and in a particular way, between the priest and the congregation.

And so, my third suggestion is this: *that the relevant section in* Redemptionis Sacramentum *be changed to allow priests and bishops celebrating Mass to leave the sanctuary, and that they be encouraged to offer the sign of peace to a few of the parishioners in the front pew.*

Proposal Number 4

There is only one mandatory committee in a parish, the finance committee. The parish priest may decide not to have a parish pastoral council, or a liturgy committee, or any other committee, but he must have a finance committee. It is mandated by canon law. In the same way, every diocese must have a diocesan finance committee.

---

5.   The Instruction *Redemptionis Sacramentum*.

It certainly says something about the priorities of the hierarchy. Whatever else is going on in the parish or the diocese, the finances must be in order.

I am not denying that mandatory finance committees are a good thing. Of course, both the parish finances and the diocesan finances need to be looked after. But so too, do the people. And there should be the same sense of urgency and care about the pastoral aspects of the parish as there is about the financial aspects.

In the years immediately after the Second Vatican Council there was an explosion of parish committees and councils as the laity became far more involved in the life of the Church at the local level. Some bishops even formed diocesan councils, and were able to dialogue directly with the laity in their diocese. Over the following decades, however, papal enthusiasm for the Council waned. The ideas and the vision of the Second Vatican Council were being openly questioned by many of the clergy, and slowly there was a return to more traditional parish structures, with the priest tending to make decisions by himself, rather than in consultation with parishioners.

I must say I am surprised by the number of priests who do not want, and do not have, parish councils. I think part of the problem might be that because of the shortage of priests, and the extra demands it has placed on parish priests, it just all gets too hard. Certainly, it is easier and far less time-consuming to make decisions yourself, rather than coming together with a group of parishioners and working through the issues. Nobody likes meetings, and all that they entail, including writing up minutes, follow-ups, and the rest. But surely the parish deserves as much.

If the parish priest is not allowed to make financial decisions about the parish without first consulting with members of a finance committee, then I feel it is only right that the same parish priest should not be allowed to make pastoral decisions about the parish without first consulting with members of a pastoral council. Ultimately, both committees are advisory only. But the consultation is important, not only because better decisions will come out of it, but because the process is important. It shows a real connection between the clergy and the laity at the local level.

This parish dynamic also holds good at the diocesan level. The bishop who puts in place a diocesan pastoral council is showing a real connection with those in his diocese, to say nothing of the knowledge and wisdom he will be exposed to in the process.

And so, my fourth suggestion is: *that there be an expectation in the diocese that all parishes have a pastoral council that meets regularly, as well as an expectation that the bishop set up a pastoral council at the diocesan level.*

Proposal Number 5

The housekeeping arrangements in presbyteries regarding such things as washing, ironing, cooking and cleaning, vary from parish to parish. Traditionally someone has been employed, either full-time or part-time, to perform these tasks, leaving the priest to concentrate on his work. While in more recent times some individual priests have taken on some, or even all of these tasks, it would be fair to say that in many cases, and probably the majority of cases, priests still have these domestic chores done for them by someone else.

The argument has always been that the priest, or bishop, needs to be able to spend his time on priestly work, rather than on these menial jobs. The work of the priest is too important, so the argument goes, for him to be spending time cleaning and ironing. It is true that most priests and bishops are busy people, and are always looking for more time to do that extra job, but they are not the only busy people in the world. Indeed, most people these days are busy, and many are working longer hours than the clergy, but the washing and ironing still needs to be done, and they don't have someone coming in to do it for them.

An integrated life involves doing a whole range of jobs, from the most exciting and challenging, to the most mundane and routine. They all have their place, and they all contribute to one's perspective on life. For the priest, who has the notion of service at the heart of his ministry, surely a little domestic work is most appropriate.

And so, my fifth suggestion is this: *that there be an expectation in the diocese that all priests, unless too old or too frail, do some basic housekeeping. At the minimum, this should involve washing their own clothes, and cleaning their own private living area.*

Proposal Number 6

The new translation of the Mass has been in use since Advent 2011. It was greeted with very little enthusiasm from both clergy and laity.

The main criticisms fall into three broad categories – its awkward style, its old style theology, and the use of words that are unfamiliar to parishioners.

The clumsy style of the language comes from the fact that it has been translated too literally from the original Latin. This is why it is often referred to as a 'latinised' version of English, because the syntax follows more closely the Latin style, rather than the English style. Hence you have long, complex sentences, sometimes with phrases and clauses that seems to be out of place. It not only makes it difficult to work out the meaning of the prayers, but it is also distracting, as you get caught up in the grammar and syntax, instead of focussing on the meaning of the prayer.

With regard to the theology behind the new translation, many argue that it takes us back to the 'bad old days' of fear and guilt. For example, in the penitential rite at the beginning of Mass, we used to say 'I confess . . . that I have sinned through my own fault in my thoughts and in my words, in what I have done and in what I have failed to do'. This was not a literal translation of the Latin. There was an attempt to move away from what is sometimes referred to as 'Catholic guilt'.

With the new translation, however, we have gone back to a literal translation, and we now say "I confess . . . that I have greatly sinned, in my thoughts and in my words, in what I have done and in what I have failed to do, through my fault, through my fault, through my most grievous fault'. It is not hard to see how this renewed emphasis on sin and guilt is concerning for many people. There is particular concern about the effect it will have on children.

The third criticism relates to the vocabulary of the new texts, and particularly those words that are seldom used in English conversation, even by those who have English as a first language. Words such as 'consubstantial' and 'oblation' are often cited as examples. While this shortcoming in the translation may not be as serious as some of its other deficiencies, one still must ask the question why words that are unfamiliar to the majority of those in the congregation would be included in what is the high point of the Church's communal prayer.

If the new translation was originally received with a lack of enthusiasm, it must be said that in the years since, not much has changed. Neither the clergy nor the laity has warmed to the text. The same criticisms remain, and even at the highest levels, there are calls for something to be done.

In March 2014, Archbishop Wilton Gregory from Atlanta, in the United States, spoke about the new translation of the Mass at a conference on 'Celebrating the Anniversary of the Constitution on the Sacred Liturgy', held in St Petersburg, Florida. Archbishop Gregory was president of the United States Conference of Catholic Bishops from 2001 to 2004, and chair of the Bishops' Committee on Liturgy from 1991 to 1993, so he has some expertise in the area of liturgy. At the conference he made this insightful observation on how to respond to the issue of the new translation. 'What we need to know, after a period of time living with it, come back and say, not, "We told you so", which I think a lot of pastors want to say, "We told you not to do that", but to say, "It's inadequate for this reason, that reason, this reason; we've tried it, we've lived it, we think it needs correction."'[6]

That 'correction', of course, means another translation. It would certainly be a lot of work, but it is certainly also possible. So much of the work is already done. We have the older translation with its freer interpretation and more contemporary style, and the new translation with its more literal and disciplined approach. There is a middle ground that keeps faithful to the Latin texts, while at the same time not losing the charm and rhythm of the English language. In fact, there is a model for this "middle-ground" translation already.

In the new Roman Missal which contains the new translation of the Mass, there are, in total, ten eucharistic prayers. The first four are the most well-known. They are commonly referred to as eucharistic prayers I, II, III, and IV. Then there are two eucharistic prayers for reconciliation, and four eucharistic prayers for use in Masses for various needs. These last six eucharistic prayers are relatively modern prayers, some of them being written and approved only in the 1970s. It is true that they were recently re-translated, in keeping with the style of the new translation of the Mass, but because these prayers are not translated from ancient Latin texts, they do not have the awkward structure of the first four prayers. In fact, for the most part, they are quite beautifully written. They still include some rarely used words and phrasing, but they are certainly not characterised by the latinised grammar of the new translation. The style of these more

---

6. Archbishop Wilton Gregory, question and answer session following his address at the conference 'Celebrating the Aniversary of the Constitution on the Sacred Liturgy', 29 March, 2014, St Petersburg, Florida, transcript by 'Pray Tell'.

contemporary eucharistic prayers, therefore, really does represent a middle ground translation, and thus a model for another, and hopefully more permanent translation, which would bring both clergy and laity closer together as a worshipping community.

And so, my sixth suggestion is: *that the bishops ask Pope Francis to establish a working committee, including both clergy and laity, to look at the possibility of producing a new English translation of the Mass.*

Proposal Number 7

The exclusion of women from the lay ministries of acolyte and reader is one of the most puzzling decisions that the Church hierarchy has taken.

Let us take a closer look at how it has come about.

Prior to the Second Vatican Council, those preparing for ordination received what was known as minor orders, before they received the major orders of deaconate and priesthood. These minor orders included the two ministries of acolyte and reader. Then in 1972 Pope Paul VI issued the apostolic letter *Ministeria Quaedam*[7] by which the minor orders were suppressed in the Latin rite, allowing the roles of acolyte and reader to be exercised by the laity.

Pope Paul goes to great lengths to make the point that the ministries of acolyte and reader are lay ministries, quite separate from ordained ministries. The conferral of the minor orders, he says, 'will not be called ordination, but institution. Only those who have received the deaconate, however, will be clerics in the true sense, and will be so regarded. This arrangement will bring out more clearly the distinction between clergy and laity, between what is proper and reserved to the clergy and what can be entrusted to the laity.'

However, when Pope Paul uses the term 'laity', he is not referring to the whole of the laity, but only to laymen. He makes it clear that these ministries are not to be entrusted to laywomen. His reason for doing so is, to say the least, rather curious. 'In accordance with the ancient tradition of the Church', he states, 'institution to the ministries of reader and acolyte is reserved to men'.

---

7. Apostolic Letter *Ministeria Quaedam* promulgated by Pope Paul VI, 15 August, 1972, St Peter's, Rome.

But that ancient tradition of the Church had just been changed. If the two ministries are no longer reserved to those preparing for priesthood, surely it is logical to suggest that the two ministries are no longer reserved to men. There is certainly no theological reason why women cannot be entrusted with the ministries of acolyte and reader, or indeed with any lay ministry in the Church. But still, forty-five years later, the ruling persists. Women are still not able to be instituted into either ministry.

In practice, the situation has become a bit messy. The bishops obviously find themselves in an awkward position, trying to argue why women should not be able to exercise these lay ministries, especially as women far outnumber men in terms of active participation in the Church. In trying to deal with the problem they have come up with two interesting responses.

First, with regard to the ministry of acolyte, the bishops have said that it is permissible for women to act in the role, provided they do not call themselves acolytes. They suggest that the terms 'senior altar servers', or just 'senior servers', would be appropriate. When there is a ceremony of institution of acolytes, however, only the men are instituted.

The situation with regard to the ministry of reader is even more complicated. It would be very difficult for the bishop to officiate at a ceremony of institution of readers, because he could only institute the men, and most of the people who read at Mass are women. The bishops' solution to the problem is not to institute anybody, men or women. If a parish wants to have some sort of formal welcoming of new readers, including the women readers, they are permitted to have a simple blessing ceremony which would not involve the bishop.

Sadly, this whole issue exposes a clergy club mentality that constantly struggles with the question of women's participation in the Church. Here is an opportunity for the bishops to do something positive for women in the Church, as I am sure they would like to. The fact that they have gone to such lengths to try and work around the ruling, suggests that they are uncomfortable with the current arrangement. I do not think it would be difficult to bring about change in this matter, particularly with Pope Francis' open and inclusive attitudes.

And so, my seventh suggestion is: *that the bishops put a proposal to Pope Francis to issue a new instruction on the ministries of acolyte and reader, allowing women to be formally instituted into the two ministries, along with men.*

Proposal Number 8

I was once going through some files in the parish office and came across a number of financial records that had been kept by the previous parish priest. They had been written up by hand in ledgers, documenting every transaction that had taken place in the parish, month by month.

I was very thankful that things had changed by the time I came to the parish. No longer did the parish priest have to do the book-keeping. We were able to employ people who had the expertise to look after the financial matters of the parish, as well as most of the administrative work.

But there was one thing that had not changed. The parish priest was still the only person who could pay a bill or sign a cheque. Even just the basic day-to-day payment of parish bills could not be done by the bookkeeper.

Once when I was preparing to go on annual holidays I contacted the chancery to see if there was any possibility that I could authorise the parish secretary to pay the bills while I was away. I was in a small parish at the time, and the supply priest would only be coming on weekends to do the Sunday Masses, and he was not keen on having to do any administrative work. The chancery staff were sympathetic to my situation, but still nothing could be done. Only a priest could operate on the parish accounts. And it is still the case today.

Obviously, I can understand the bishop's concerns regarding parish finances, and his desire to keep them tightly controlled. But there is another issue involved here, and that is the issue of trust, trust between the clergy and the laity.

It should not be the case, but sadly it seems to be, that the real measure of trust in a relationship comes down to money, the willingness of one party to trust the other with the finances. In the case of the parish, there seems to be an unwillingness on behalf of the clergy to trust the laity to administer the parish finances with prudence and honesty.

I don't know why this should be the case. I do not think there is any evidence to suggest that priests are either more prudent, or more honest, in dealing with financial matters. Certainly, in my own experience I can say that every parish staff member that I have worked with has been a person of the highest integrity and trustworthiness. In any case, there are many checks and balances that can be put in place to ensure appropriate oversight.

It is interesting to note how much trust is put in parish staff and volunteers in other areas of parish life. Sacramental coordinators are entrusted with the care of our young children, as are the catechists. Parish youth workers are entrusted with the care of our teenagers. Pastoral care coordinators are entrusted with the care of the sick and the aged. Ministers of the Eucharist are entrusted with the Blessed Sacrament. And yet none of them is able to sign a cheque.

If this practice were to change, it would be a powerful symbol of the trust the clergy are prepared to show in the laity, in all areas of parish life.

And so, my eighth suggestion is: *that the parish priest be allowed to authorise a member of the parish to operate on parish accounts for parish business.*

These are my eight suggestions, eight practical ways to put in place policies that will help break down the barriers between clergy and laity. The proposals are modest and unthreatening, but that means they are doable. Bishops may have other suggestions for achieving the same goals, and that would be wonderful, but I would find it hard to understand why at least some of these proposals could not be tried. How could anyone argue that the laity and the clergy should not meet together to discuss important Church matters, or that priests and bishops should not have to undergo any sort of appraisal process, or that women should be excluded from lay ministry. I cannot see any sort of harm that could result from any of these eight proposals, but I can certainly see a lot of good that would come out of them.

Conclusion

Many people write books about the Church. Many of those books are quite critical about various aspects of the Church. Many of the people who criticise the Church are active members of the Church, and have been all their lives. So why don't they just accept the fact that the Church is what it is, and is probably never going to be the Church they hope for?

The answer is simple. It is because they love the Church, and want it to be the best Church it can be. They may not be happy with some aspects of the Church. They may not agree with some of its practices. But it is still their Church, the faith community they belong to, and are bonded to.

It is a bit like one's family. If someone has differences with other members of the family, and if there are tensions that seem difficult to overcome, one does not say, 'I think I'll go and find another family, a family that thinks more like me'. You may well find another family that you get on better with, but it's not your family.

In this book, I have been critical of what I perceive as clericalism in the Church. I have described it as a 'club' mentality. I have gone to great lengths to argue that this club mentality is not the fault of individual priests and bishops, but rather it stems from a culture that pervades the whole of the ordained ministry, and is firmly entrenched in it. As a priest myself, I have not only seen this mentality at close quarters, but I am also part of the problem. I have struggled constantly, and not always successfully, to eradicate clericalism from my own ministry, and to dismantle the barriers that disconnect the clergy from the laity.

I know many people will not be happy that I have criticised the Church. I know many within the clergy will see me as 'breaking ranks'. I can only refer to my earlier example, and say that the Church is my family, and like every other committed member, I want it to be the best Church it can be, and at the moment I don't believe that is happening.

At this time in the Church's history there is a need for people to speak out, and try to address the ailments that are preventing the Church from flourishing as it should. Pope Francis himself has certainly not shied away from doing this. As I have already noted, he is particularly critical of what he calls 'sicknesses' or "diseases" of the clergy, such as 'spiritual petrification', 'spiritual Alzheimer's disease', 'the disease of idolizing superiors', and 'the disease of indifference to others'.

Currently the Church is going through a very crucial period in its history. While one might see huge crowds gathering in St Peter's Square, and hundreds of bishops celebrating Mass with the Pope, that doesn't tell the whole story. Statistically the Church is plateauing. The 2016 Pontifical Yearbook records the total number of Catholics in the world as increasing by .05% from 2005 to 2014, relative to the increase in world population.[1] It also describes the growth in the number of priests over the same period as 'stable'. In the most recent statistics published on the number of seminarians in major seminaries around the world, they show a slight fall each year from 2011 to 2014.

When looking at statistics for the Catholic Church one always has to be mindful of the fact that the numbers are much better for the Church in the developing countries, particularly in Asia and Africa, and much worse for the Church in the wealthier countries, such as in Australia, and many countries in Europe. Historically the poorer countries have kept the overall numbers increasing, but that trend seems to be changing. And the numbers won't get any better for the Church, because as the poorer countries continue to develop and become wealthier, the Church in those countries will have to deal with the same issues that it is currently dealing with in Western countries, issues that are bringing about both a decline in the number of Mass attenders, and a decline in the number of those training for the priesthood.

---

1. Pontifical Yearbook 2016 and the *Annuarium Statisicum Ecclesiae* 201 Dynamics of a Church in Transformation, 5 March 2016.

What is the reason for this decrease in numbers? Why is it that the Catholic Church is not flourishing as it has in the past, particularly in the Western world? These are questions that have been asked many times and will continue to be asked. Everyone has an opinion, and every commentator has a different perspective.

Certainly, there are some obvious reasons, such as the clergy sexual abuse crisis, the rise of modern day atheism, and the widespread loss of confidence in traditional institutions generally. But there is another reason why I feel people are becoming more and more disenchanted with the Church, and it's the topic of this book, the club mentality of the clergy.

Ultimately, it is people's day-to-day-experience of the Church that determines whether they remain committed and involved, or drift away. Pope Francis may be extraordinarily popular, but the fact that people like him, will not necessarily translate into higher Mass attendance. Far more relevant is the relationship that people develop with their parish, whether or not they feel a sense of belonging, whether they find it easy to get to know other parishioners, whether they feel their faith is being nurtured and stimulated. And in that regard the priest, as leader in the parish, has an extremely important role to play, and must accept some responsibility if the parish is not flourishing.

Just as the Pope sets the tone for the universal Church, so too the parish priests set the tone for the local parish communities. If the parish priest is welcoming, the parish is known as a welcoming parish. If the parish priest is inclusive, the parish is known as an inclusive parish. If the parish priest is friendly, the parish is known as a friendly parish. And, of course, the reverse is also true. If the parish priest is rigid, frosty, and unwelcoming, the parish is seen in the same way.

Over the years I have been involved in an endless number of seminars and conferences, and private conversations with priests, about how the Church is faring, and how it will continue to fare into the future. As diocesan priests, we are particularly interested in the parishes, and how they are doing. Of course, we often talk about the fact that numbers are falling off, and how the once full churches are now half-full, or even worse. In all those discussions it is very rare, extremely rare, to hear a priest or bishop say, 'We, as the clergy, have to take some responsibility for the situation'. Instead, it is always someone else's fault. 'The parents are not giving good example'. 'The Catholic schools are not teaching the proper religion'. 'Society has lost its sense of morality.' But the reality may well be that the clergy has lost its ability to connect with the laity.

Some may argue that the model of priesthood that I am proposing is not a valid model. It is too secular. It is too much 'with the laity'. It is not in keeping with the priest who is 'set apart'. I am very aware of those positions. Indeed, the 'set apart' model was the model of priesthood I grew up with, and in which I was initially trained. But it is a model that leaves itself open to clericalism, and to a club mentality, and, as I have tried to show in this book, it is a model that stifles the initiative of the laity and creates a Church with two levels of membership.

None of us knows what lies ahead for the Church into the future, either in regard to its growth, or in regard to what it will look like, centuries, or even decades from now. Certainly, new ways of doing things will be tried. The traditional model of individual parishes, run by male, celibate priests, has served the Church well in the past, but it is debatable whether this model will continue to serve the Church into the future. But no matter what changes are made to better express the mission of the Church, no matter what new models are incorporated to better proclaim the message of the Gospel, one thing is for certain, and that is that the Church will only fulfil its enormous potential when the laity and the clergy work together as one, when they are on the same footing regarding their importance and their sacredness, and when all forms of clericalism are gone, and there is no longer any trace of 'clubishness' remaining in the attitudes and the behaviour of Catholic bishops and priests.

Glossary

Acolyte
Minister assisting a priest or bishop during liturgical celebrations

Advent
A period of approximately four weeks prior to Christmas during which Christians wait expectantly and prepare for the celebration of Jesus' birth

Altar breads
Wafer like discs made from wheat that are used for Holy Communion in the celebration of Mass

Anointing Mass
A special Mass during which the sacrament of the Anointing of the Sick is administered

Anointing of the Sick
Sacramental rite administered by a priest to bring spiritual and physical strength during illness

Archbishop
Bishop of a higher rank or office

Archdiocese
Larger or historically significant diocese of an archbishop

Assumption
Feast day 15 August celebrating the Catholic belief that God took Mary body and soul into heaven

Auxiliary Bishop
Bishop assigned to assist the archbishop with pastoral and administrative roles in the archdiocese

Benediction
Blessing of the congregation with the Eucharist contained and exposed in a special vessel

Bishop
Senior member of the clergy, often in charge of a diocese, and empowered to administer the sacraments of Holy Orders and Confirmation

Canon Law
Ecclesiastical or Church law decreed by papal pronouncement for the governance of the Church and its members

Cardinal
Leading dignitary of the Church and member of the Sacred College that elects the Pope

Cassock
Ankle length, loose outer garment worn by clergy and others having a role or office in the Church

Chalice
Large wine cup or goblet used on the altar during Mass to hold the wine before and after consecration

Chancery
The administrative office of the archdiocese

Chasuble
Long, sleeveless, ornate outer vestment worn by a priest when celebrating Mass

Chrism Mass
Often celebrated on the morning of Holy Thursday for priests and bishops to celebrate, among other things, the unity of the priesthood.

Ciborium
Container with lid used on the altar during Mass to hold the bread, before and after consecration

Clerical
Constituting or relating to the clergy. Can also have a pejorative sense implying a preoccupation with clergy affairs.

Clergy
The ordained members of the Church - deacons, priests and bishops

Communion Rite
Culmination of the liturgy of the Eucharist, comprising the Lord's Prayer, the Sign of Peace, the Breaking of Bread, Communion and the Prayer after Communion

Concelebrate
Two or more priests or bishops celebrating Mass together

Confirmation
Sacrament of a special outpouring of the Holy Spirit to complete the initiation rites into the Catholic Church

Consubstantial
Of the same substance or essence with reference to the three persons of the Trinity in Christian theology

Council of Priests
A committee of priests and auxiliary bishops who act as an advisory body to the archbishop

Deacon
Man ordained to the diaconate either as the final step before ordination to the priesthood or as a distinct and permanent vocation

Deanery
Group of parishes presided over by a regional dean who is a cleric

Diaconate
Intermediate or permanent ordained office providing a range of liturgical and pastoral ministries

Diocese
Geographical area under the pastoral care of a bishop

Ecclesial
Constituting or relating to the Church

Episcopate
The office of bishop, attained through Holy Orders, by which the fulness of the sacrament is conferred

Eucharistic Minister
Can refer to either the priest (ordinary minister of the Eucharist) who celebrates Mass, or the lay person (extraordinary minister of the Eucharist) who helps with the distribution of Communion at Mass and takes Communion to the sick and elderly

Eucharistic Prayer
Structured prayer of remembrance, offering and thanksgiving prayed during the liturgy of the Eucharist

Eucharistic Sacrifice
Commemoration of the Lord's Supper through the offering of bread and wine, by which Catholics remember the sacrifice of Jesus on Calvary

Eulogy
Testimony given at a funeral often by a family member or friend commemorating the life of the deceased

Hierarchy
Ranking of ordained ministries according to status and authority – deacon, priest, bishop, cardinal, Pope. Can also be used to refer to all ordained ministers in the Church, although sometimes refers only to the bishops

Holy Communion
Participation in the Eucharist or Lord's Supper when the consecrated bread and wine are distributed among the people and consumed. Can also refer specifically to the consecrated bread and wine

Holy Orders
Sacrament that confers ordained status as deacon, priest or bishop

Host
Term used to signify the presence of Jesus in the consecrated bread

Incarnation
Christian belief that Jesus is both human and divine

Laity
All members of the Church who are not ordained

Latin Mass
Older form of the Mass known as the Tridentine Mass, celebrated in Latin, as distinct from the modern-day Mass which may also be celebrated in Latin

Latin Rite
Liturgical rites used by that part of the Church originating where the Latin language once dominated, and often referred to as the Roman rite. It is numerically the largest of the rites and unlike other rites, priests of the Latin rite are bound by a rule of celibacy.

Lay Ministers
Work carried out by the laity for the Church community, usually on a volunteer basis eg catechist, musician, acolyte

Lent
Period of approximately forty days from Ash Wednesday to Holy Thursday during which Christians prepare for the celebrations of Holy Week and Easter

Levite
Member of the Jewish tribe of Levi who assisted the priest in temple worship

Limbo
Place of those who died before Jesus came, as well as those unbaptised but not deserving of punishment, such as infants

Mitre
High headdress worn by bishops as a symbol of office

National Council of Priests
Australian wide organisation of Catholic clergy who join together to support each other in their priestly ministry, and to offer services to the wider Church. Founded in 1971

Oblation
Presentation of bread and wine to God in the sacrificial offering of the Eucharist

Ontological Change
The change in the nature of one's existence or being that is believed to take place through the sacrament of Holy Orders

Opus Dei
Institution of the Catholic Church founded in 1928 in Spain. The majority of members are lay people committed to holiness in daily professional life as the 'Work of God'.

Penitential Rite
Part of the introductory rite of the Mass during which the congregation pray for forgiveness

Pharisee
Member of an ancient Jewish sect distinguished by strict observance of traditional and written religious laws

Pope
Head of the Roman Catholic Church and Bishop of Rome

Presidential Chair
Particular chair on the sanctuary where the presiding priest or bishop sits during some parts of the Mass

Purgatory
Temporary place or state of spiritual cleansing following death

Rabbi
Jewish scholar, teacher of Jewish law and leader of worship

Reader
A lay reader trained and assigned to read a biblical text other than the Gospel at Mass

Reconciliation
Sacramental rite by which Catholics are reconciled to God and to each other

Religious Orders
Communities of men and women who live by the principles of their founders in the form of vows, commonly obedience, poverty and chastity

Rite of Christian Initiation of Adults (RCIA)
Program by which people who are not baptised, but are interested in becoming Catholic, are gradually introduced to the beliefs and practices of the Catholic Church before being invited to receive the sacraments of initiation.

Rites of the Catholic Church
Church traditions about how the sacraments are to be celebrated. There are many different rites within the Catholic Church, such as the Maronite rite, the Melkite rite, the Ukrainian rite and the Latin rite.

Roman Curia
Papal court and government departments of the Vatican

Rosary
Form of personal or communal devotion using a string of beads to count a series of short repeated prayers while reflecting on the mysteries of the Catholic faith

Sacristy
A room in a church where the clergy vest and where the sacred vessels and vestments are kept

Samaritan
Native or inhabitant of Samaria, a region west of Jordan

Scribe
Ancient Jewish record keeper, theologian and jurist

Seal of Confession
The obligation placed on a priest to keep confidential what is told to him in Confession by a penitent

Second Vatican Council
Gathering of Catholic bishops of the world, and others, from 1962 – 1965, which brought about significant change in the policies and practices of the Church

Sign of Peace
Community greeting of peace and unity shared among the members of the congregation and the priest at Mass, immediately before Communion

Soutane
Ankle length outer garment worn by clergy

Third Rite of Reconciliation
Sacramental rite used in special circumstances during which the priest gives a general absolution of sins and penance after the community has privately reflected and repented

Vatican II
An abbreviation for Second Vatican Council

CPSIA information can be obtained
at www.ICGtesting.com
Printed in the USA
FSHW020232030619
58661FS